Awaken Optimism

**366 Meditations for Making
Each Day Amazing
Gregory Barton**

Special thanks to all the authors who have been quoted in this book. The entries for each day of the month begin with a quote and attribution. My use of the attributed authors' quotations is solely for the purpose of providing my own comments on the quotations. Any errors or omissions, typographical errors, etc., are not intended.

Table of Contents

Dedication

For my son, Tyler Barton. I love you more than you can possibly know.

For my parents, Jimmy and Martha Barton, who taught me to be the best version of myself that I could be. I love you both so much, I owe you everything, and I miss you terribly.

Support clean drinking water. I'm proud to offer 10% of all author royalties as a donation to those on a mission to improve the world, including CharityWater.org, where 100% of donations go to support clean drinking water projects in a world where far too many people live without clean drinking water.

Acknowledgments

I could not have completed this work alone. Luckily, I had a little help from my friends. I owe so much too so many.

I want to take a moment to acknowledge those who have had a positive impact on me.

To my family. To my mother, thank you for being one of the strongest people I ever knew. To my father, I wish we had been closer. To my sisters, who were always jealous of the baby brother, still love you anyway. Thank you both for your love and support. To my son Tyler, I am so very proud of you and the man you are. Thank you, and I love you all very much.

To my office staff, Leslei and Jazin. You have been critical in my mission to bring this project to life. Thank you, thank you, thank you. You do so much for me, and you're always optimistic and cheerful. Thank you for your steadfast dedication, hard work, and contributions. I owe you so very much.

To my closest and dearest friends and associates who helped me proofread this book and who gave me incredibly honest, valuable feedback. You are my inner circle. Your support means more than I can say. I will be forever in your debt.

To everyone who I have ever worked with. Whether you know it or not, you have made a tremendous impact on me. I have learned so much over the years, and I am so thankful for all the experiences and challenges. I can't thank you enough. Working with each one of you has had a lasting impact on my thoughts, my work, and my life.

To all my fellow members of the armed forces of the United States, including the Navy, Marine Corps, Army, Air Force, Coast Guard, Army National Guard or Air National Guard, and Space Force. It was the honor of my life to serve among you all. I've been there, and I'm with you in spirit. Thank you for doing what you do every single day and every night. Thank you for doing far more than you are paid for. Thank you for being willing to endure dangers that few will ever understand. Thank you for being hyper-vigilant, on watch or on patrol at sea, under the sea, in the homeland of our great nation, on foreign soil of our allies or adversaries, in the air, or behind enemy lines. You and I both know that 99% of what you do never makes it to the news. Thank you for every sleepless night, every drop of sweat, every tear from yourself or from your loved ones who are missing you terribly. Thank you for dealing with sleep deprivation, miserable conditions, and all the other arduous challenges that you face. You are our best and brightest. Our entire nation owes you more than we can ever pay. Thank you from the bottom of my heart. I am grateful for all you do to keep us all safe.

To my clients, thank you for allowing me the opportunity to bring value to your organization. I have a strong reputation of being honest, doing the hardest jobs, taking on challenges far greater than I sometimes thought I could effectively handle. It has been a tremendous journey, and I owe you all a sincere thank you.

To everyone with whom I've had any encounter. Everyone has an impact in some way. Each encounter and each relationship has had an impact that has made me the person I am. I want to say a heartfelt and sincere thank you.

To all the amazing authors whose quotes are included in the book. I view each of you as a mentor and a friend. Please accept a heartfelt and sincere thank you to each of the following authors, listed alphabetically by first name: Abraham Lincoln, Albert Einstein, Ambrose Bierce, Anne Frank, Aristotle, Audrey Hepburn, Barack Obama, Benjamin Disraeli, Benjamin Franklin, Bob Iger, Brian Tracy, C.S. Lewis, Carol Burnett, Catherine Pulsifer, Colin Powell, Confucius, Dan Millman, Daniel J. Boorstin, Darren Hardy, David G. Allen, Donna Karan, Dr. W. Edwards Deming, Duke Ellington, Elbert Hubbard, Eleanor Roosevelt, Ernest Hemingway, Estella Eliot, Franklin D. Roosevelt, Gary Johnson, Gary Keller, Gen. Rick Hillier, Goldie Hawn, H. Jackson Brown, Harvey Mackay, Helen Keller, Henry Ford, Herb Kelleher, Jack Canfield, James M. Barrie, Jan Brett, Jason Ayres, Jim Collins, Jim Rohn, Jimi Hendrix, Jimmy Buffett, Jimmy Dean, John C. Maxwell, John Wooden, Justice Sonia Sotomayor, Kathleen A. Brehony, Kenneth Blanchard, Kevin Kelly, Larry Elder, Les Brown, Lucille Ball, Lucy MacDonald, Mae West, Mahatma Gandhi, Malala Yousafzai, Malcolm Gladwell, Marcus Tullius Cicero, Maria V. Snyder, Marie Forleo, Martin Luther King Jr., Mary Lou Retton, Maya Angelou, Michael Gerber, Michael P. Watson, Napoleon Hill, Nicholas M. Butler, Noam Chomsky, Norman Cousins, Oprah Winfrey, Peter Drucker, Price Pritchett, Ray Davis, Rick Steves, Robert Kennedy, Robert Pirsig, Robert Schuller, Rohit Pandita, Ronald Reagan, Rosa Parks, Roy T. Bennett, Sam Harris, Samuel Johnson, Serena Williams, Seth Godin, Sharon Lechter, Sheryl Sandberg, Spencer Johnson, Stacy London, Stephen Covey, Steve Jobs, Theodore Roosevelt, Thomas

Edison, Thomas Jefferson, Tim Ferriss, Tom Hiddleston, Tony Robbins, Victor Hugo, Will Smith, William James, Winston Churchill, and Zig Ziglar.

I'd also like to say a special thanks to Seth Godin, for whom I have the utmost respect and appreciation. Seth is a writer and a teacher who helps people through his many books and workshops. Thanks Seth! Seth can be found on the web at www.seths.blog or www.akimbo.com. I can't recommend Akimbo more highly.

Also, I'd like to thank Brian Tracy. Brian Tracy is Chairman and CEO of Brian Tracy International, a company specializing in the training and development of individuals and organizations. Brian's goal is to help people achieve their personal and business goals faster and easier than they ever imagined. Brian can be found on the web at www.BrianTracy.com.

Last but never least. To my readers, who enthusiastically support my work, thank you so very much!

Introduction

This year, 2020 has been a year of tremendous change, uncertainty, and difficulties for so many. I never expected that I'd see a pandemic in my lifetime, but here we are. The world has changed is so many ways from what it previously was. It has been a time of terrible tragedy and sadness for so many. This year has been the year of WTH and it seems that the trend may continue for quite some time. I couldn't think of a more perfect year to try to do something that will positively impact the world, even if in some very small way.

Originally, this book started as a collection of quotes I felt where inspirational. I started this project because I felt like I personally needed a daily reminder of how to stay more positive. Things are tough sometimes and we all need reminders along the way. That was especially true this year.

It also seems as if we're trending in the wrong direction at times. As an example, the world seems far more negative today than it did five years ago. It seemed more negative five years ago than it did ten years ago. As you might guess, it seemed more negative ten years ago than it did 20 years ago. For whatever reason, it seems as though the world has become a very negative place. We all know chronically negative people. I know way too many people who see things from a pessimistic perspective and each day is a challenge for them. I want to help each one of them.

Each of us has a decision to make. What will we do to make today amazing? What will I choose? What will you choose?

What will we choose? It is up to us. We can change it if we want to. All we have to do is think about things differently.

Overall, I am very grateful and lucky. I have had the honor and pleasure of serving in the US Navy and serving as a senior leader in various healthcare organizations throughout my career. I have worked with some of the world's finest men and women in the military. I have worked with some real superstars in healthcare. I have learned so much from so many others throughout the years. Thank you all for the opportunity to serve, to grow, and to learn to become better and better each year. It has been a remarkable journey and I'm extraordinarily proud to have been so fortunate to have the experiences that I have had. There have been many challenges along the way. I have learned as much from the challenges as possible. I continue to learn each day.

As I transitioned to the civilian sector and began my healthcare leadership career, I started making some observations. I remember thinking, "Life is going to be different as a civilian." I began thinking deeply about what problems I was seeing on a daily basis. I was thinking about why those problems occurred in the first place, how we can prevent problems in the future, rather than dealing with the same or similar problems on a recurring basis. What a great idea… if we could prevent problems rather than trying to solve them, my job would be a lot easier and the people I work with would be a lot happier. It's so simple, at least in theory. As is often the case, things are a little more complex in reality. I also believe that if you have the will to do great things, you can. The world always needs more great things and if you're able to create it, you will be rewarded.

You must focus on what you want to accomplish and persist against obstacles and resistance you'll encounter along the way. I also believe it's necessary to keep the negativity in check. Sometimes, that negativity comes from others around us. More dangerous perhaps is if the negativity comes from your own thoughts. You are what you believe. So you might as well believe something good.

The work presented in this short book has been helpful to me. I hope it's helpful to you as well.

———•●•———

"The value of an idea lies in the using of it."

— Thomas Edison

For anything to be helpful, you must use it. My intent is for each of us to have something to turn to each day for guidance and inspiration. I hope you use these and I hope they help you make a greater impact within your life and in your organization.

———•●•———

Creating this work and releasing it this year has been a tremendous challenge. I'm very proud of the work I have done and the people I have encountered on this journey. I can be a bit of a perfectionist and it is difficult to release something into the world without it being absolutely perfect. I really believe that I could work on it for another year and it wouldn't be perfect. But I do believe it's good — certainly good enough to ship and stamp my name on — and the time is right putting out something good into the world. It is not perfect. There are things that I've learned in the editing process that I wish I had more time to change. But I promised myself I would get this book out this year. So, I'm keeping the promise to myself and releasing the book to the world, including all the imperfections and things I'll change for the second edition.

It is my sincere hope that I will be able to have a positive, uplifting impact on each person who reads this book and carefully considers the ideas presented. Thank you for joining me on the journey.

January

January is a new beginning. It is a fresh new start with all the optimism in the world. We have traditions of making resolutions, which sometimes become only a vague memory a few months later.

What are you most proud of having accomplished last year? What did you leave unfinished? What will you do with the gift of this new year?

———•●•———

January 1

"Consistency is the key to achieving and maintaining momentum."

— Darren Hardy

Most of us have worked with the type of people who aren't very consistent, can't meet deadlines, don't answer emails, and general don't accomplish very much in their careers. Building and keeping momentum is hard, but very worthwhile. Especially for the chosen few who accept the challenges, great reward will follow. Know it and believe it. The rewards will follow your efforts.

January 2

"Better slip with foot than tongue."

— Benjamin Franklin

In the information age and considering the widespread influence of various social media platforms, this quote seems to be a little bit out of fashion. But maybe it isn't. Have you seen someone say something dreadful on social media that they later regret? Slow down and take a moment to breathe. Pause and make sure you want to say what you're about to say. Go ahead, write that post. Just wait until tomorrow and think three times before deciding to really send it out into the world.

January 3

"Discipline is the bridge between goals and accomplishment."

— Jim Rohn

The more disciplined you are, the more you can accomplish. Gaining and keeping discipline can be challenging, but it is worthwhile. Many people prefer to make excuses rather than be disciplined and work toward the desired result. What are some areas of your life that could benefit from a greater degree of discipline? If you were to truly focus, what could you achieve this year that you've been wanting to do for a very long time?

January 4

"Develop an 'Attitude Of Gratitude'.
Say thank you to everyone you meet for
everything they do for you."

— Brian Tracy

Gratitude changes lives for the better. You can improve your life and the lives of countless others by being more grateful and showing appreciation to others.

January 5

"Don't wait. The time will never be
just right. Start where you stand, and
work whatever tools you may have at
your command and better tools will be
found as you go along."

— Napoleon Hill

Overthinking about an idea delays the execution of that idea. Worse still, your mind can play tricks on you and cause you to form self-limiting beliefs. You may never feel ready enough. But you are probably ready. Just do it and watch things fall into place. Procrastination should have no place in your life because time will pass by, and one day you will regret why you didn't do it sooner. You may find that you are more likely to regret the things you did not do, but not the things you did.

January 6

"An important part of any focusing regimen is to set aside time at the end of the day — just before going to sleep — to acknowledge your successes, review your goals, focus on your successful future, and make specific plans for what you want to accomplish the next day."

— Jack Canfield

A little self-reflection is good for your health. When you make it a habit to continually reflect on your life, you will appreciate yourself more and have a clear understanding of the future you want. This will help you understand yourself better and make better decisions.

Give yourself a gift. Take a moment. Think about the events of the last day. Think about what might be possible. Plan the next day. Then when you wake up the next day, you'll already be clear on how you want the day to go. This process takes a little time, but you'll feel more confident in your ability to get things done so you can celebrate your success.

January 7

"While anonymity can be used to protect heroes, it is far more commonly used as a way to escape responsibility."

— Kevin Kelly

The world is a better place when people take responsibility. Take ownership. Own it, make it better. Fix it and be responsible for it. You should always act responsibly. By definition, if you do not, you are irresponsible.

When you take greater responsibility, you may notice that opportunities open up to you. You can do this. You can be more responsible and get better and better each day. Get curious. In what areas can you accept greater responsibility? What might be possible if you do? What are three things you can do this week to take greater responsibility?

January 8

"There's a difference between interest and commitment. When you're interested in doing something, you do it only when it's convenient. When you're committed to something, you accept no excuses - only results."

— Kenneth Blanchard

Commitment is a superpower. Talk is cheap and people give lip service and excuses 95% of the time. But the 5% that is real commitment, that is where real magic lives and real progress is made.

———•●•———

January 9

"Change happens when the pain of holding on becomes greater than the fear of letting go."

— Spencer Johnson

Change is so incredibly difficult for most people. But, human beings are built to adapt to change. If you're like most people, you do exceptionally well with change when it is forced upon you and you don't have any alternatives. You probably adapt quickly and become quite innovative when you must.

In my experience, I've been surprised at what can get accomplished once I've embraced change and moved forward. Sometimes it is an internal drive. At other times, it takes an external catalyst. The right amount of motivation helps significantly. What if you were better equipped to view change as a positive — an improvement — and as a result, there was less resistance to it? What might be possible if that's how you viewed the world every day?

January 10

"Have the humility to learn from those around you."

— John C. Maxwell

It is usually better to learn from others. You can learn a lot by observing others. Unfortunately, that is not always possible. You will make mistakes. But, as long as you learn something, it you are minimizing the cost of the mistake.

Sometimes, when you make a mistake, that experience is indelibly etched into your mind. It is hard to forget the mistakes you have made, isn't it? Paying attention and learning from others is crucial to achievement. When you are trying to learn from the mistakes of others, you should consider that they either failed to plan, didn't effectively execute, or perhaps their timing was off. It pays to learn all you can when someone else is paying the price.

January 11

"We see the world not as it is, but as we are."

— Stephen Covey

Billions of people inhabit the world. All of whom have been raised differently and have diverse views of life. It influences us in many significant ways. One's perspective of an individual situation or even life, in general, is different from another person's perspective. For this reason, it is good to accept everyone as they are, despite differences in perspective.

January 12

"There is nothing so useless as doing efficiently that which should not be done at all."

— Peter Drucker

Wasting time is no good. It is pointless to waste time on things that are not necessary. Before doing things, ask yourself, "is this really necessary?" Should it be done at all? Would this be better handled by someone else, or perhaps scheduled at a particular time in the future? If you eliminate all the time wasted on things that shouldn't be done, you might find you have plenty of time for your must do items.

January 13

"None of us can change our yesterdays but all of us can change our tomorrows."

— Colin Powell

You can't run from the past, nor should you. Everyone makes mistakes. It is inevitable that you will make a bad decision on occasion. The important thing is to try to learn from it. It is difficult to move forward while still holding on to the past. Try not to dwell. When you accept the past, you'll be more free to choose to make tomorrow better. Move on and focus on your tomorrow. Strive to learn the lessons and forgive yourself so you can boldly move forward.

January 14

"Tomorrow becomes never, no matter how small the task, take the first step now."

— Tim Ferriss

Procrastination is a weakness that many people have. It is very easy to put things off and postpone the things that could be done today. When you have something to accomplish, do it as soon as possible. Otherwise, things will pile up and you'll get behind. The cost may be that you never get to achieve the things you want. What have you been procrastinating on? How much of a difference would it make if you either accomplished it today, or made significant progress so that it could be accomplished in the next day or two?

January 15

"You must never be fearful about what you are doing when it is right."

— Rosa Parks

Doing the right thing can be quite uncomfortable. You should remember that you must do what's right, no matter how difficult. Making the right decisions can come with challenging consequences. But, there is no greater satisfaction than doing what is right.

———•●•———

January 16

"There has never been and never will be another you. You have a purpose — a very special gift that only you can bring to the world."

— Marie Forleo

Each of us screams uniqueness. Our individuality is what makes us exclusive. Love and accept yourself. There's only one YOU, make it count.

———•●•———

January 17

"Speak when you are angry and you will make the best speech you will ever regret."

— Ambrose Bierce

When you get angry, the most important thing you can do is delay before responding. It is also the most difficult thing to do. The easy thing is to react and say what's on your mind.

Anyone can do that. It makes you small. Often, it leads to terrible outcomes that could have been avoided.

January 18

"In the end, it's not the years in your life that count. It's the life in your years."

— Abraham Lincoln

Are you really living up to your potential? Are you doing meaningful work that really matters? Are you proud of your accomplishments? Do you enjoy the people who you're surrounded by?

January 19

"There is no education like adversity."

— Benjamin Disraeli

Adversity is an excellent teacher. When things don't go as expected, you have a couple of basic choices. You can just give up. Many do. Or you can pivot and try again.

My recommendation is that you try again. Keep trying. Don't give up. Lean forward and press on despite the resistance. Is it easy? Well, no, of course not. But you'll be glad that you did.

January 20

"The easiest thing is to react. The second easiest is to respond. But the hardest thing is to initiate."

— Seth Godin

You can react, but that can result in trouble because it is more of an immediate, emotional response. You can respond, which is better because it allows you to pause for a moment and switch from the emotional reaction to more logical and sound thinking. You can make a giant leap forward when you initiate.

Learning to be proactive and take the first step towards something great — the initiation of it, and moving forward in a spirit of cooperation and teamwork — is a truly worthwhile effort.

January 21

"The very long tail of the future is already here."

— Kevin Kelly

To some degree, the future seems uncertain. On the other hand, you can see a little bit about the future if you pause for a moment to think about it. The future is filled with unlimited possibilities. Technology has made opportunities available that have never existed in human history. The advances in technology have brought the future to our present. The question is, what are we doing with it?

Does your present involve mindless consumption of social media, television, gossip, or other distractions? Or, are you using your present to learn more and have a better life? What will you do today and for the rest of this week that will make a difference in your own life one year from today?

$$\sim\!\!\bullet\!-\!\bullet\!-\!\bullet\!\sim$$

January 22

"You look at where you're going and where you are and it never makes sense, but then you look back at where you've been and a pattern seems to emerge."

— Robert Pirsig

Everything becomes more apparent in hindsight. As you look back at things that have happened, it becomes a lot easier to connect the dots, and figure out why something happened that seemed particularly mysterious at the time when it happened to you. What will you do with the insight you gain from looking back? What differences will you plan in your future?

January 23

"Change almost never fails because it's too early. It fails because it's too late."

— Seth Godin

Change is inevitable. Why is there so much resistance to it? I believe that change is more likely to be good than bad. That is how I choose to see it. If you view change as an improvement, then there is no valid reason to resist it. You can't simply wish it away or pretend like change isn't happening. It is. It always has been. It always will be.

When you embrace change with a spirit of optimism and with the right amount of positive energy, you open your mind to new opportunities. You will find that things flow more naturally, and things just seem to come together in ways you may not have thought possible.

What are the changes you see on the future horizon that you're most excited about? What may be possible when those changes are entirely in place? How do you anticipate that others around you will feel about the change? What can you do to support those around you? Can you offer strength to others who may be struggling?

———•●•———

January 24

"How to apologize: Quickly,
specifically, sincerely."

— Kevin Kelly

If you are progressing forward in life, you will most certainly make mistakes. You should realize that you are not perfect, that you are human, and permit yourself to make mistakes.

Have a strategy for dealing with your own mistakes. Take responsibility. Own it. Apologize sincerely for them. It is not easy, but it is always worthwhile, and it means something to those who really care and who we care about most.

———•●•———

January 25

"Sometimes it's a little better to
travel than to arrive."

— Robert Pirsig

Have you ever accomplished a goal and felt a little let down at the end, having seemingly less energy than you had along the way prior? The fun part is the journey along the way. It's great getting to the destination, but the trip is often the part that makes us feel most alive and satisfied.

January 26

"Optimism is a happiness magnet. If you stay positive, good things and good people will be drawn to you."

— Mary Lou Retton

The law of attraction is alive and well. I think of optimism as energy. The more optimistic you are, the more energy you will have. The more good energy you send out into the world, the more good energy you will receive in return. This is a free gift that you can receive each day. It is there for you. All you need to do is to give generously and then open yourself to receive all the good things in store for you. Most importantly, don't forget to be grateful.

January 27

"When we give cheerfully and accept gratefully, everyone is blessed."

— Maya Angelou

Each of us can help someone with something. By helping others, you will feel better about your contributions. When you help others, you will make a positive impact that lasts far longer than you imagine. Who will you help today?

January 28

"Strong people don't put others down...
They lift them up."

— Michael P. Watson

You have a choice to make. Do you use our power for good and bring positive energy, or do you become a force of negativity and destruction? You can create the impact you want as long as you decide and commit. You will be stronger when you help others. Who will you help lift up this week?

January 29

"Be aware of little expenses; a small
leak will sink a great ship."

— Benjamin Franklin

Optimistic thoughts are like deposits into your bank account. Negative thoughts are like expenses from your bank account. Negativity is cancer.

Life is like a long voyage on a ship. You need to be aware of any negative thoughts, so you don't sink the ship. It would be best if you took care of the ship in order so you can arrive safely.

Negative thoughts are more damaging than you realize. They are invisible and affect your beliefs, which affect your behaviors, actions, and results. Choose optimistic thoughts instead.

January 30

"Optimism is an attitude and a choice. It involves context and focus."

— Seth Godin

Your thoughts are always present. Your thoughts can be helpful or they can hold you back. Remember, you do have a choice. You can choose how you proceed. Once you decide and commit, you will think different thoughts, act differently, and get different results.

What results do you want to bring about this year? What differences are required in your thoughts to get those results?

January 31

"Be the change that you wish to see in the world."

— Mahatma Gandhi

Change is unavoidable. The future is about change. To resist the change is an exercise in waste. To embrace the change and work to assure that it is a positive change is a worthwhile exercise. It is an investment into the future. You have the ability. All you need to do is make the choice, to decide, to commit with your energy and enthusiasm, and to boldly work for a better tomorrow.

February

February is the month of love and includes Valentine's Day. February is also Black History Month. Mardi Gras is often in February but sometimes falls in March.

Have you looked back at January? After reflection, what did you get accomplished that was most meaningful? What were some disappointments? How will you make February different? Remember, February is a short month, so think about that now and make sure you make the most of it.

February 1

"Losing is a habit. So is winning. Now let's work on permanently instilling winning habits into your life."

— Darren Hardy

If both winning and losing are habits, why not choose winning? Sure, you may not always win. But if you don't have the goal to start with, it's difficult to imagine that you'll ever accomplish much.

February 2

"People are entitled to joy in work."

— Dr. W. Edwards Deming

Most work that I have done has provided me with a lot of enjoyment. Sure, there are difficult days and circumstances. Often, difficult people with their own toxic beliefs or behaviors. Ultimately, the choice is up to us to be joyful and do a great job.

February 3

"The best way to predict your future is to create it."

— Peter Drucker

Are you really able to create your future? Are you in control of your destiny? Without question, you can find people to argue these points. What is true is that you have so much within your control. What if you just focus on that and try to make things better as much as you can? Doing this hour by hour, day by day, month by month will yield amazing results.

February 4

"He that would live in peace and at ease, must not speak all he knows nor judge all he sees."

— Benjamin Franklin

What might you receive if you act with purpose and intention while choosing to be less judgmental? What if you were more open to possibility? Would you be happier and have more peace of mind? Why not give it a try? You might be surprised at what you find.

———— • ● • ————

February 5

"Learning is the beginning of wealth. Learning is the beginning of health. Learning is the beginning of spirituality. Searching and learning is where the miracle process all begins."

— Jim Rohn

Life is a constant learning process. Learning and growing and developing ourselves continues throughout our lives. When you've stopped learning or you just don't want to put forth the effort, look out!

———— • ● • ————

February 6

"Live your life in every way to earn and keep the respect of the people you respect."

— Brian Tracy

We all need other people. When you are disrespectful, the world will respond in kind. If you respect others and act honorably, you will be proud and have less regret. Strive to respect others and to be respected in return.

February 7

"Life is really simple, but we insist on making it complicated."

— Confucius

I have observed that human natures sometimes leads us to make things more complicated. Knowing that is important. You need to be intentional. Make things as simple as possible. Consider the question, "how can I simplify this?" Then try it and see if you like it. What can you simplify this week? What might be possible if you did?

February 8

"For every reason it's not possible, there are hundreds of people who have faced the same circumstances and succeeded."

— Jack Canfield

There is nothing new under the sun. Everything that you are going through has happened to other people before you. You would do well to remember that in every hard situation that you have, you will make it through it. There is no reason to give up, and you must push through all difficulties. You must not give up. You will overcome the challenges that you face if you recognize that those who were before you went through the same situations.

February 9

"**The greatest obstacle to discovery is not ignorance – it is the illusion of knowledge.**"

— Daniel J. Boorstin

Knowledge can be great. Is it possible to have too much knowledge? Some would argue there's no such thing as too much knowledge. I'm not sure I agree with them. Might it be possible that the things you know with certainty stifles your curiosity? Could it be preventing you from being creative at times?

Say yes to curiosity. Don't allow knowledge to stifle your curiosity or creativity. What are you most curious about? Could you reflect on your curiosity and come up with some creative new thoughts? Imagine what you could discover.

February 10

"**Vision is knowing who you are, where you're going, and what will guide your journey.**"

— Kenneth Blanchard

You were born for a reason. None of us is here on earth to live our lives without a purpose. When one loses their sense of meaning, they feel less fulfilled. Their lives will have less direction. Find your purpose. Maintain that sense of purpose and have a clear understanding of where you are going in life. Move towards your goals and never give up.

February 11

"**Finding inner success is the best, easiest and in fact the only way to achieve and enjoy everything else in life.**"

— Spencer Johnson

As much as you need other people in your life, you must always be aware that you need your best self much more. You may seek to please others and maintain a peaceful rapport with them, but do you have inner peace? Look deeply within yourself. When you accept yourself fully, you will be happier and live a better life.

February 12

"**The secret of your success is determined by your daily agenda.**"

— John C. Maxwell

Most people say you should take life one day at a time. That is good advice. If you have goals (and you should), work on them daily. We are all different. Have a plan for your day.

When you do something daily, it gradually becomes a habit. You'll be more successful and achieve more if you do.

February 13

"You're not a product of your nature. That is your genetic makeup or your nurture, the things that have happened to you. Of course those things affect you powerfully, but they do not determine you."

— Stephen Covey

You make decisions. You get a result based on your decisions. You are the result of the decisions you've made today and in the past. Making decisions can be a bit complicated in our modern world. Things seem to be getting more complex as each day passes.

But you would do well to pause and remember. You do have a choice. You can decide to make different choices. What will you choose today? What would be possible if you made new choices? How would that make you feel?

February 14

"Efficiency is doing things right; effectiveness is doing the right things."

— Peter Drucker

It is good to strive for perfection. But, what exactly are we striving to be perfect at? We aim to do things well at all times, but we must be cautious that our attention is not on the wrong things. If we do things that are not right, they will be a waste of time, no matter the effort we put in them. Legitimate success is in doing the right things the right way, the first time.

Oh, and Happy Valentine's Day!

February 15

"If the challenge we face doesn't scare us, then it's probably not that important."

— Tim Ferriss

Most people avoid challenges and changes. That is why there are only a handful of successful people. Success requires the courage to face the things that you fear most — the fear of the unknown. When you have goals that are a bit frightening, pursue them. If your goal is easy to achieve, and it is not much of a challenge, then ask yourself if you have the right goals. What are your current goals?

February 16

"I have learned over the years that when one's mind is made up, this diminishes fear; knowing what must be done does away with fear."

— Rosa Parks

You can never pursue anything wholeheartedly if you are not entirely on board. Before putting your time and energy into something, it is best to set your goals and stick with it. Nothing can stop anyone who has made their mind to achieve something. Trying to stop them will be like trying to stop the earth from rotating — impossible.

February 17

"Not having the best situation, but seeing the best in your situation is the key to happiness."

— Marie Forleo

Perspective plays an essential role in our lives. How you choose to see a particular situation contributes a lot to how you handle it. If you see hard times as moments that wear you down, then they will wear you down. If you see them as opportunities to grow, then you can push through them with a positive attitude.

———•●•———

February 18

"You don't have to control your thoughts. You just have to stop letting them control you."

— Dan Millman

What if you allow your thoughts to simply flow through you like water flows gently down a stream? What if you were to pick out and try to hold on only to those thoughts that have the greatest possibility to improve your life and the lives of those we care most deeply about? Do you believe that is possible? What might happen it you tried it for a week to see how it goes? Will you try it?

———•●•———

February 19

"A challenge only becomes an obstacle when you bow to it."

— Ray Davis

Eagerly accepting challenges and meeting those challenges head-on is an exciting way to be the conductor of our own symphony.

February 20

> "If it's not relevant, it's noise. If it's untrusted, unwelcome or selfish, it's noise."
>
> — Seth Godin

You have the ability to be relevant and trusted. You have a choice in how you show up and present yourself to the world. Discovering that and learning to be the best version of yourself is fun and rewarding. It's something that you and ONLY you can do.

You get to make a decision and then act on it. You can choose to be specific, not vague. You can choose to be personal and warm, not cold. You can choose to be more relevant tomorrow than you were today. You can show up with generosity and reject selfishness. What will you do this week to make sure you're part of the signal, not the noise?

February 21

> "Evolution doesn't care about what makes sense; it cares about what works."
>
> — Kevin Kelly

Often, I find myself wondering "why" about things. In the end, does it really matter? From my perspective, what has a greater impact is if we get curious and ask, "what if _____?" Try a simple experiment and see what happens. If you understand what activities lead to a given result, then all you have to do is do those activities, and you can expect that you will have a similar outcome.

Consider a mentor, role model, or a coach. They can help give you great support. If you're wondering what really works, someone else out there has already figured it out. You just have to find that person that can help support and guide you.

When was the last time you asked for assistance from someone who knows what the answer is and has already gone down the path that you are considering? What would be possible if you tried?

February 22

"Quality is a direct experience independent of and prior to intellectual abstractions."

— Robert Pirsig

Your work's quality says a lot about you, who you are, what you value, what you think about, and how you use your time and energy. Are you focused enough on quality? Is your work great, or does someone have to double-check all your work and continuously find errors or things that must be corrected? If so, is that level of quality acceptable to you? What are some things you can do to improve the quality of your work?

February 23

"If you want to dig a big hole, you need to stay in one place."

— Seth Godin

If you want to move forward in life, you have to keep moving. Staying in one place is not the answer. Venture into the unknown. Move forward. Be an agent for change and improvement. You have the power of choice. What will you choose today?

February 24

"If you are not falling down occasionally, you are just coasting."

— Kevin Kelly

Don't be afraid to fall. Just move forward. Just keep moving. Press on and do what you can to help make a positive difference in the world. Yes, you will make mistakes, and you will fall. But, jump right back up and get back in the game!

February 25

"The past exists only in our memories, the future only in our plans. The present is our only reality."

— Robert Pirsig

It is essential to have learned from the past. Equally important is taking the opportunity to use your imagination and daydream about the future. But, living in the present is a real gift. The here and now is where you are, and there is a certain calmness that is available when you recognize that you are fully present. Are you being fully present? If not, what will you do to be more present?

February 26

"Optimism inspires, energizes, and brings out our best. It points the mind toward possibilities and helps us think creatively past problems."

— Price Pritchett

Almost anything is possible if you believe that it is. Only when you believe that things are possible can you truly accomplish them. It doesn't take any extra energy to have an open mind than it does to have a closed one, so why not give it a chance? Maybe others will join in.

February 27

"If someone doesn't value evidence, what evidence are you going to provide that proves they should value evidence."

— Sam Harris

Facts and evidences are important. They matter more than opinions. With technology, facts are easier than ever to find. But so is misinformation.

You should remember to make sure that you're paying more attention to facts than opinions. Then, you can draw some conclusions. But you must remember that a conclusion based on evidence may be true, but then again, it may not. You can also draw false conclusions. Spend some time thinking about this and you may find some relevance. Will you take the time to rely more on facts than opinions? What might be possible if you did?

February 28

"The best way to predict the future is to create it."

— Abraham Lincoln

You may find that having a vision about a possible future that you would like to create is more challenging than in years past. Life today is filled with endless distractions, problems that are competing for our attention, and things that take us far off the track of where we're trying to go.

This is why it is important to stop, reflect on the past, and daydream about the future. You should remember that almost anything is possible and decide what you will do to bring your vision to life. What future will you create?

February 29

"My mission in life is not merely to survive, but to thrive."

— Maya Angelou

When you survive, you are just working to make it through — just to get by. But, when you thrive and live up to your potential, you get so much more out of the journey. You should ask yourself, "am I surviving or am I thriving?"

If your answer is that you are surviving, you could choose to get really curious and explore the reasons why. Perhaps it is a result of situations that are outside your control, which is sometimes the case. But maybe it's that you have been influenced by outside forces or your innermost thoughts and you have allowed yourself to form self-limiting beliefs.

What is possible, if you alter your thoughts, choose to believe, think new thoughts, act upon new choices, and see what kind of results you might be able to achieve? The outcome may just surprise and delight you beyond imagination.

March

March is the third month of our year. March is famous for containing International Women's Day and Saint Patrick's Day.

How many resolutions are still in place? How many have been abandoned or forgotten? What will you do about that? Let's make March amazing!

———•●•———

March 1

"Small, Smart Choices + Consistency + Time = RADICAL DIFFERENCE."

— Darren Hardy

The little things really do add up. It's natural to underestimate the downstream results that can be achieved with the right amount of action and consistency. The difference one person can make when they are consistent and persistent is inspiring to me.

———•●•———

March 2

"In the End, we will remember not the words of our enemies, but the silence of our friends."

— Martin Luther King Jr.

We have to stand up for what we believe in. Talk is cheap, actions speak louder than words. Everyone needs support, encouragement, and to be pushed forward. Which of your friends can you positively influence today?

March 3

"Experience teaches nothing without theory."

— Dr. W. Edwards Deming

Experience is very important. But so is the understanding of where things fit. By understanding different theories, we broaden our minds and create more opportunities for ourselves and the future that is possible

---

March 4

"Knowledge has to be improved, challenged, and increased constantly, or it vanishes."

— Peter Drucker

Things change, and change quickly. Especially in the modern world, it is more important than ever to use the knowledge we have, add to it, work through things that need to be corrected, and work toward continual improvement. That is the only way to make a better world. What will we focus on improving today? What can we do today that will make the biggest impact on tomorrow and next week? What if we scheduled those things on our calendar and then make sure they get done?

———•●•———

March 5

"**Wish not so much to live long as to live well.**"

— Benjamin Franklin

What is more important to you, longevity or a life well lived? What areas of your life fall short of being well lived at this moment? What will you do to change that?

———•●•———

March 6

"**The challenge of leadership is to be strong, but not rude; be kind, but not weak; be bold, but not a bully; be thoughtful, but not lazy; be humble, but not timid; be proud, but not arrogant; have humor, but without folly.**"

— Jim Rohn

We will accomplish the most when we are strong, resilient, kind, thoughtful, humble, and keep a sense of humor. Which of these do we need to work on improving today?

March 7

"It doesn't matter where you are coming from. All that matters is where you are going."

— Brian Tracy

We have all come from different backgrounds. For some of us, that may be seen as a disadvantage, that we look at our past instead of the promising future. Well, in this life journey, our past matters less. What matters most is what is ahead of us and where we are heading to in life. Forget the past, and focus on the future.

March 8

"You can't heal what you don't acknowledge."

— Jack Canfield

Acceptance is the beginning of change. When we want to change something within us or around us, we must first accept its existence. This way, we will be able to comprehend the problem and find the appropriate solutions to it. If it is a weakness, a bad habit, a bad condition at the office, whatever it is, we must first accept then act.

March 9

"Integrity is telling myself the truth. And honesty is telling the truth to other people."

— Spencer Johnson

The truth is always a hard pill to swallow. Not many people can bear to handle the truth when it gets exposed before them. Those who can handle the truth are strong people that can overcome anything. This is more so if the truth involves them. Better yet is someone who speaks the truth as it is, without sugarcoating it. Such people may seem hard on others, but they are a blessing.

March 10

"Feedback is the breakfast of champions."

— Kenneth Blanchard

Communication is essential in every relationship. It is very discouraging to talk or pass a message to someone that gives no feedback. It is worse, especially for businesses. Feedback ensures growth, as you would get various perspectives from different people. Without feedback, one cannot know which action to take. Thus, there will be a lack of growth.

March 11

"Talent is a gift, but character is a choice."

— John C. Maxwell

We were all born with a gift. Some of us were lucky enough to realize our talents at a young age, while others are still working on finding it out. With innate gifts, we can soar to greater heights. However, it is our character that will guarantee how long we stay at those great heights.

March 12

"Greatness is setting ambitious goals that your former self would have thought impossible, and trying to get a little better every day."

— Tim Ferriss

Most of us have big dreams, some of which we fear pursuing. Fear, when not dealt with, can keep us stagnant. But, if we choose to pursue those goals no matter what, we will be surprised how much we can grow. So, set the goal you want to achieve, do something about it daily, and see how far you will go.

March 13

"You wouldn't have the dream if you didn't already have what it takes to make it happen."

— Marie Forleo

Everyone's dream is unique. No one can clearly understand a particular dream more than the dreamer. When we have a dream, we already have the tools we need to achieve the dream. So, do not be afraid to pursue a dream that you have. Instead, pursue it with all that you got because you already have what it takes to get to achieve it.

March 14

"I've learned that making a living is not the same thing as making a life."

— Maya Angelou

These days, a lot of people are more focused on making a living instead of making a life. A lot of people are after better lives, wealth, and luxurious assets. Well, this does not make life complete. We should focus on having good lives, lived in love and peace with those around us. We must seek to have a positive impact on ourselves and on those closest to us. What would be possible if everyone of us did this every day?

March 15

"Do you want to know who you are? Don't ask. Act! Action will delineate and define you."

— Thomas Jefferson

I'm curious about how our nation's founding fathers would feel about the ways the world has evolved. As an example, there is more information and knowledge available to us today than they may have been able to imagine.

Taking effective action was favored centuries ago and I believe it is still favored today. Knowledge is good, but action gets results. What actions are you planning to take this week? How will they define you? What might you need to adjust in order to be the best possible version of yourself?

March 16

"Patience is the calm acceptance that things can happen in a different order than the one you have in mind."

— David G. Allen

Sometimes the order of things is critical. As an example, when we are cooking, the order of things is essential, as is the temperature. How and when we add ingredients matter. It can make all the difference in the outcome. At other times, there may be less of a need to be critical or controlling. We may find that by easing up a bit, we get more accomplished with less effort. Others may feel empowered by easing up as well. Ultimately, our goal is to get better outcomes, where the people involved get more meaning, greater satisfaction, and more fulfillment.

———— • ● • ————

March 17

"Expectations are the engines of our perceptions."

— Seth Godin

What we perceive to be happening in the real world is influenced strongly by our expectations. If we have positive expectations, we are more likely to see positive things happening. When we see positive things happening, we feel gratitude and look for opportunities for more positive things to be happening in the future as a result. This becomes a cycle. It becomes a cycle of optimism. We will in turn find more and more positive things happening to us in the future as a result of us expecting positive things to happen. Therefore, more positive things do happen to us. Could it really be that simple? What if it is? Why then, would anyone choose to have a negative expectation about something? Clearly, it doesn't make much sense.

March 18

"Clearly, we are self-made. We are the first technology. We are part inventor and part the invented."

— Kevin Kelly

Once we realize that we all have the power of choice and that it can influence, to a large degree what happens in our present and our future, then we open the world of possibilities. What future do we want? It's important to know how to attain it. It's even more important to clearly define it and understand what it is that we want. Then, and only then, we take a significant step towards a better tomorrow.

March 19

"To live only for some future goal is shallow. It's the sides of the mountain that sustain life, not the top."

— Robert Pirsig

The destination may be the top of the mountain. But the side of it is where the journey happens — the experiences of proceeding step by step with our faith and beliefs about continuing forward. The destination is just a focal point, but the real magic happens all along the way through all the difficulties, overcoming all the obstacles through the continuous effort. We believe it is the destination that we want, but it is indeed the journey that makes it worthwhile.

March 20

"Big ideas are little ideas that someone killed too soon."

— Seth Godin

No doubt, it can be a bit discouraging when we have what we think is a good idea, and when you tell someone, they will tell you why it's not a good idea, won't believe its potential, or they won't feel the same. Perhaps they're not meant to. They can't possibly see it from your perspective. How could they?

Only you can see things how you see them. There is only one you in the world, and you are unique and have your own perspective and experiences. This is the lens through which you see the world.

Do you have an idea that you think will make an impact? Act on it. The world needs more ideas and more people acting in a way to make things better.

March 21

"Pros are just amateurs who know how to gracefully recover from their mistakes."

— Kevin Kelly

Why is our society so against making mistakes? What if we had a culture where mistakes are more readily accepted, and we encouraged each other to share our error with others and what we learned from it. What if this approach would generate better outcomes?

March 22

"Optimism is a strategy for making a better future. Because unless you believe that the future can be better, you are unlikely to step up and take responsibility for making it so."

— Noam Chomsky

Everyone has the power to make something better for someone else. What will we choose to do better today? Who will we make it better for? Who will we need assistance from to improve?

March 23

"Be fanatically positive and militantly optimistic. If something is not to your liking, change your liking."

— Rick Steves

Being and staying positive makes a difference each day. This attitude is contagious, and can spread and help others. How much positivity can we spread today?

March 24

"Act as if what you do makes a difference. It does."

— William James

We all have choices. Few people truly understand just how powerful of a thing that is in our present and for our future. What we think and what we do really matters. We all have more power than we can imagine.

March 25

"If someone doesn't value logic, what logical argument would you invoke to prove they should value logic?"

— Sam Harris

We all need to remember that we can use logic or we can use emotions. Emotions usually win. Often, they will pass and we would have been better served making logical choices, not choices based on our feelings at that moment.

March 26

"It doesn't matter how slow you go, as long as you don't stop."

— Confucius

Keep moving forward. It has worked for centuries. It will work today. What would be possible if you developed persistence found by only a few?

March 27

"Always bear in mind that your own resolution to succeed is more important than any other one thing."

— Abraham Lincoln

We should remember that we also must decide upon our definition of success. We need to get really clear on what the definition of success is to us. Only then will be able to move courageously forward and see the dream come to life.

March 28

"Each person must live their life as a model for others."

— Rosa Parks

We can all do something to help serve the needs of someone else. If nothing else, how we live our lives serves as an example for others to see, and choose if they're interested in doing so. We must decide what we're going to stand for and make choices in alignment with our decision.

March 29

"Try to be a rainbow in someone else's cloud."

— Maya Angelou

We can each make a positive impact on someone else. Sometimes, the others won't notice or appreciate it. They're too caught up in their own circumstances or their own overwhelm to stop and notice. That's OK. Do it anyway. It is worth the effort and the universe will rewards us for our efforts.

March 30

"Life is like riding a bicycle. To keep your balance, you must keep moving."

— Albert Einstein

Just keep moving. Don't stop. When you think you've gone as far as you can, just take one more step, then another, and then another. Lather, rinse, and repeat. Do it again. Again. Again. Repetition is the path to success. Forward progress, now and always. Just keep moving. You can do it! We all can!

March 31

"If we want to succeed, we need to recover our grandparents' work ethic."

— Darren Hardy

We all realize that things change over time. Sometimes, our priorities change as we grow older. It seems that with time, the work ethic in general has changed significantly though. What if we could inspire others to have a better work ethic by demonstrating an excellent work ethic ourselves? What could we help the world get accomplished by providing a clear, positive example for others to emulate?

April

April is famous for April Fool's Day. I fondly recall the saying, "April showers bring May flowers."

April is the beginning of the second quarter. We've made it through Q1 and we have an opportunity to start with a new quarter. What were some of the most meaningful things that happened in Q1? Is the year progressing as you want? What adjustments will you need to make? What might be possible if you make those adjustments?

April 1

"Most of us spend too much time on what is urgent and not enough time on what is important."

— Stephen Covey

There is an important distinction between what is important and what is urgent. We need to focus on the things that important to us. The things that are urgent for others shouldn't dictate our work. People who spend too much time on what is urgent fail to realize what is important and usually accomplish very little of significance. Rather than face this reality and change themselves, they often seek to criticize others, probably to protect themselves from the reality of their misdirected efforts.

April 2

"Change is inevitable. Growth is optional."

— John C. Maxwell

We can all control how we view change. Since we can't avoid it, wouldn't it be better for us to simply embrace change and prepare to deal with it in the way that helps us achieve our goals? By achieving our goals, we grow and learn every step along the way.

April 3

"The first step toward change is awareness."

— Darren Hardy

We can't change the things for which we have no awareness of. Being present and aware is prerequisite for growth.

April 4

"Every man must decide whether he will walk in the light of creative altruism or in the darkness of destructive selfishness."

— Martin Luther King Jr.

Without question, selfishness is an expression of negative energy. Will we be selfish and negative? What would be possible if instead we acted with incredible generosity? After all, like most things, it is nothing more than a decision that we make. That decision must be followed by action. What generous action will you take today?

April 5

"The aim of leadership should be to improve the performance of man and machine, to improve quality, to increase output, and simultaneously to bring pride of workmanship to people."

— Dr. W. Edwards Deming

In the work that you do or in the organizations where you contribute, what improvements are needed in personnel, equipment, quality, and output? What are some things you can and will do today to begin making those improvements?

April 6

"Management is doing things right; leadership is doing the right things."

— Peter Drucker

So much has been written on leadership and management. In a world with so much information, it is surprising how there can be so many powerful examples we see in poor leadership and management practices. How can we improve or positively influence the practices of leadership and management?

April 7

"Start your day with why, then get on with your what."

— Darren Hardy

When we have a clear understanding of our WHY and start our day with it, it can serve as a constant reminder during the day for things that arise that aren't in alignment with our WHY. If we can spot things that don't align and prioritize them appropriately before we get caught up in a whirlwind of competing priorities, we have a better chance of getting accomplished the things that are most important for that day.

April 8

"He that falls in love with himself will have no rivals."

— Benjamin Franklin

Love is more powerful than hate. If we love ourselves, we bring good energy to the world. Good energy attracts other good energy to us. With good energy, almost anything is possible. Imagine a world with more love, less conflict, and more true goodness. What are two things you will do today to express love for yourself and start changing the world for the better in the process?

April 9

"Excuses are the nails used to build a house of failure."

— Jim Rohn

Most people are looking forward to better lives and better things. But, what stops those who achieve their goals from those who do not is being persistent. A large number of people tend to give up on their dreams along the way and give excuses for quitting. Well, if we use reasons for leaving on stuff, we will never accomplish anything in life.

April 10

"Your most valuable asset can be your willingness to persist longer than anyone else."

— Brian Tracy

Persistence is critical in everything we want to achieve, from the daily goals to those that will take years. Life can cause us to give up on our dreams sometimes. But, we must keep on working towards what we want by doing something about it every day. We must push through towards our goals. Giving up is not an option.

April 11

"You have to break free of your past to discover yourself and you have to discover yourself to create a future."

— Michael Gerber

No one can escape their past. It is an integral part of our lives that we cannot avoid. For us to move on to the future, we must be willing to let go of the past. As hard as it is, we cannot move forward when our history is still haunting us. We must learn from it, let go, and embrace what the future has for us.

April 12

"You don't hire for skills, you hire for attitude. You can always teach skills."

— Herb Kelleher

It's surprising how much people lie in their resumes. Managers have had tough times deciding whom to recruit in their staff. Well, the best way to sieve out incompetent job candidates is by checking their attitude. Someone may have the best skills but the worst temperament. Nobody wants that.

April 13

"Don't quack like a duck, soar like an eagle."

— Kenneth Blanchard

Anyone who wants to be successful must be willing to do extraordinary things. If we get used to doing the usual things, we will get typical results. But extraordinary actions bring remarkable outcomes. Like eagles, we must be willing to soar to greater heights, which are meant only to those ready to fly to those altitudes. Strive to achieve your goals no matter what it takes.

April 14

"Peace is not the absence of conflict, it is the ability to handle conflict by any means."

— Ronald Reagan

No matter how much people love and adore one another, conflict sometimes springs out of nowhere. We must, however, not let disagreement come between us and cause unrepairable damage. Learn when to concede, swallow your ego, and apologize.

April 15

"Focus on impact, not approval."

— Tim Ferriss

A lot of people have different reasons for doing different things. Most, however, act based on getting other people's approval. It will feel good at first, but the feeling will wear out after a while. It is best to do things to create an impact, instead of having people to praise you. The effect it creates lasts longer. Approval is short-term, a momentary bliss.

April 16

"The measure of our lives is not determined by what we achieve for ourselves; it's determined by what we share, give, and contribute to others."

— Marie Forleo

"Blessed is he that gives than he who receives." Every bit of this statement is true. We may be after our goals and better lives for ourselves and those we love. This is good: however, more satisfaction comes by serving others. When you have a habit of sharing and giving, you will be more content and happier than the wealthiest man on earth.

April 17

"My mission in life is not merely to survive, but to thrive; and to do so with some passion, some compassion, some humor, and some style."

— Maya Angelou

Maybe someone has ever told you, "Don't take life too seriously." It is not a consoling statement, especially during challenging times, but it can be helpful. When we go through life with a survivor mentality, we will not achieve much.

However, if you live a life full of passion, humor, and some panache, then boy, you will have a lot to live for!

— • ● • —

April 18

"Find the minimum amount of technology that will maximize your options."

— Kevin Kelly

Picking the right tools can make dramatic changes in productivity and give better results. Choose wisely.

— • ● • —

April 19

"When you reach the end of your rope, tie a knot in it and hang on."

— Franklin D. Roosevelt

Sometimes we have to just ride out the storm. We know it won't be fun, but there isn't much of an alternative. We will get past this and be stronger and more capable than ever before. Are there areas where you're getting near the end of your rope? Be strong and be ready to accept the challenge.

April 20

"In our desire to please everyone, it's very easy to end up being invisible or mediocre."

— Seth Godin

Most of us understand that it is impossible to please everyone all of the time. Why waste the energy? The better use of our time and energy is to figure out who we're trying to please and then figure out what we think will please them. Are we trying to please others? Or, are we trying to please ourselves? Who should we be trying to please? Why? What if we give ourselves permission to get curious and consider that we have an opportunity to make different choices. What might be possible if we do this each day?

April 21

"A vacation + a disaster = an adventure."

— Kevin Kelly

Life is one big adventure. Sometimes it's more fun than others. If we learn to enjoy the journey, it is a much better experience. What kind of adventure have you had thus far? What kind of adventure would you have over the next year if anything were possible? What will you do about it?

April 22

"If someone's ungrateful and you tell him he's ungrateful, okay, you've called him a name. You haven't solved anything."

— Robert Pirsig

Name-calling solves nothing. The real work begins when we try to solve problems. Calling names does nothing. Identifying problems and also trying to work with others to achieve real solutions, now that is something worth putting your energy, focus, and attention into. What types of problems are you working to solve today? Who might you need help from in order to achieve those solutions? If you got those solved, what else might be possible?

April 23

"Leadership is scarce because few people are willing to go through the discomfort required to lead."

— Seth Godin

Those who think leadership is easy most likely have never had real responsibility. There are many critics, many opinions, many perspectives, and many judges. It's easy to sit back and criticize, but the real work and the most meaningful progress comes when you step forward and are willing to put others ahead of your own agenda and lead others. It isn't easy, but it is very worthwhile. It is an honor and a pleasure to lead, particularly when you were leading a fabulous team.

━━━━●•~~~

April 24

"When crisis and disaster strike, don't waste them. No problems, no progress."

— Kevin Kelly

There is no shortage of problems in the world. There is no shortage of opinions in the world. There is no shortage of judges in the world or those who criticize and critique. There is, however, a shortage of solutions. The shortage isn't because answers are not available, but rather because solutions require effort and energy. Many people aren't willing to put forth the energy necessary to find a solution and see it through.

━━━━●•~~~

April 25

"An optimist understands that life can be a bumpy road, but at least it is leading somewhere. They learn from mistakes and failures, and are not afraid to fail again."

— Harvey Mackay

What if we viewed the bumps as a sign that we're learning, growing, and becoming something better than before? The bumps and potholes are signals that we're moving forward. They aren't signs to slow down or turn around. We should learn, but just keep moving forward. What we're doing is too important to be put off or discarded.

April 26

"I am enjoying my life because things aren't going the way I planned."

— Rohit Pandita

How boring would life be if everything went strictly according to plan? Be present and enjoy the journey!

April 27

"You are never too old to set another goal or dream a new dream."

— C.S. Lewis

Age is really only a number. Pursuing things we are passionate about with an open mind helps keep us moving forward and keeps us thriving.

April 28

"When you are asked if you can do a job, tell 'em, 'Certainly I can!' Then get busy and find out how to do it."

— Theodore Roosevelt

There's a lot to be said for having a can-do attitude. Having a willingness to take on something and do great — especially when you really didn't know how — can be exciting and invigorating. You'll most likely find out along the way that you know more than you thought and that you're far more capable than you ever dreamed.

April 29

"Almost all our suffering is the product of our thoughts. We spend nearly every moment of our lives lost in thought and hostage to the character of those thoughts."

— Sam Harris

Understanding how we think and learning to improve our thinking process is really important if we want to enjoy the present and create a better future. What future will you create? How will you feel when that future becomes the present?

April 30

"Optimism doesn't wait on facts. It deals with prospects."

— Norman Cousins

The things that are possible in the future are often only limited by our imagination. It is easy to get trapped into trying to connect the dots of facts of the past (or even perceived facts) and determine what can or cannot be done. But we should be aware of this. We can all be biased in a way that doesn't help us create a compelling future vision. Being aware of this, is the first step. Keeping aware of it is something that is helpful to remember each day. Taking time to daydream about what is possible in the future is something that we usually don't spend enough time doing.

May

May is fun because of the Cinco de Mayo celebration. On a more somber note, it includes Memorial Day to honor our nation's fallen. Please, take a moment to remember the fallen.

How is your year shaping up? What has been the central theme of your year thus far? What has been your greatest accomplishment? In what areas do you need to put more energy? Think of the possibilities if you do and if things go well. What might be different by the beginning of next month if you really focus?

May 1

"I am not a product of my circumstances. I am a product of my decisions."

— Stephen Covey

Why do we not teach decision making skills? The ability to make good decisions is highly sought after and is in short supply. Making better decisions yields better results. Isn't that something that would benefit us all?

May 2

"Stay focused instead of getting offended or off track by others."

— John C. Maxwell

Maintaining the ability to not take things personally is worth the effort. While not easy, it is worthwhile and pays big dividends over time.

May 3

"There's nothing wrong with ordinary. I just prefer to shoot for extraordinary."

— Darren Hardy

Anyone can be ordinary. Why not put forth a little extra effort and stand out above the crowd? Extraordinary results come from regular people who strive for excellence instead of making excuses or playing the blame game.

May 4

"Rarely do we find men who willingly engage in hard, solid thinking. There is an almost universal quest for easy answers and half-baked solutions. Nothing pains some people more than having to think."

— Martin Luther King Jr.

Easy answers that people want to be true sell millions of products every year. We each have the opportunity to think through things, educate ourselves, and use our minds to achieve bigger and greater things. Who can we inspire today to do more thinking and do more great work that will yield meaningful results in the future?

May 5

"Follow effective action with quiet reflection. From the quiet reflection will come even more effective action."

— Peter Drucker

Reflection is so important for us to assess progress. Not only can it make us feel good to have awareness of the things that we have accomplished, but it can also help us spot opportunities for becoming more effective in the future. Since change is impossible without awareness and desire, this reflection is key to our development.

———————•●•———————

May 6

"Everyone is affected by three kinds of influences: input (what you feed your mind), associations (the people with whom you spend time), and environment (your surroundings)."

— Darren Hardy

As humans, we are influenced by virtually everything. Now would be a good time to take a moment and think about what we are putting into our minds, who we are hanging around with, and what are environment looks and feels like. What if we were to make some improvements in each of those areas? How would that look? How would that make us feel? What are we going to do about it?

———————•●•———————

May 7

"Well done is better than well said."

— Benjamin Franklin

We all have probably heard the sayings that talk is cheap, and actions speak louder than words. It is generally helpful to talk about things with people to make sure your ideas are clear and sound, and also for planning and coordination purposes. But pass those few situations, getting things done is far better than talking about it. What are some things that you have been talking about doing, but haven't done? What will you get accomplished today and this week to make a difference?

May 8

"Life does not get better by chance, it gets better by change."

— Jim Rohn

"By changing nothing, nothing changes." Tony Robbins nailed it on that one. Nothing comes by loafing around and waiting for it. If there are situations that make us uncomfortable or unhappy, it is up to us to get up and do something about it. We cannot afford to miss out on the good things that come about when we make changes for the better.

May 9

"There are no limits to what you can accomplish, except the limits you place on your own thinking."

— Brian Tracy

Why would we place limits on ourselves? It doesn't seem logical, does it? Perhaps we've learned through experiences or through socialization or through our upbringing that we have limits. We've somehow learned that when we go pass our limits, something causes us to snap right back to them again. Maybe it's criticism or comments from family members, friends, or co-workers. But, instead of being confined within those limits, what if instead we acted with courage and bravery and believe we are limitless? What if we acted as if we were limitless in order to see what might be possible? What kind of experiment will you do this week to test if you have limits beyond those that we've allowed to be placed upon us? How energized will you feel once you find out that your limits are far beyond where you previously thought?

May 10

"If you do not know how to ask the right question, you discover nothing."

— Dr. W. Edwards Deming

Questions are powerful and a great way to learn, uncover potential, opportunities, and understanding in a deeper, more meaningful way. When we discover things, we see opportunity and the path becomes more defined.

May 11

"I believe the difference between great people and everyone else is that great people create their lives actively,

```
while everyone else is created by their
   lives, passively waiting to see where
          life takes them next."
```

— Michael Gerber

It is a choice. A decision. Decide, then act. Be open to alternatives and other points of view, but do not be closed off by naysayers, just believers, or your own self-doubt. Only you can be you, and only you can bring about into this world what you've been put here for. Do it with confidence and passion. Believe.

May 12

```
"A company is stronger if it is bound
      by love rather than by fear."
```

— Herb Kelleher

Fear really has no place in the modern workplace. Managers who attempt to coerce, power-jockey, manipulate, or intimidate others are a toxic force. They should be discarded from the company with reckless abandon. Toxicity is alive and well in companies small and large. Nonetheless, the companies that embrace optimism, positivity, a can-do positive attitude will dramatically outperform those that attempt to control their workers through management by fear tactics. What would be possible if we all contributed because we wanted to, rather than because we were afraid of what would happen if we did not?

May 13

"Trust, but verify."

— Ronald Reagan

Trust is earned. It does not come easy. Let us not be quick to approve of someone or something immediately. It is best to check twice and ensure that they are worth your trust. Trusting easy has got many people in trouble. But, it is not going to be us. Complete verification before trust is highly necessary for anyone seeking peace and success in life.

May 14

"Success can usually be measured by the number of uncomfortable conversations we are willing to have, and by the number of uncomfortable actions we are willing to take."

— Tim Ferriss

The road to success is not easy. Many say that it is paved with many failures. If we are unwilling to go through these awkward positions while pursuing our goals, we can as well kiss success goodbye. Embrace the good and the bad.

May 15

"The most powerful words in the universe are the words you say to yourself."

— Marie Forleo

We can be our own best friends or worst critics. What we tell ourselves influences us in a lot of the things we do. Let us cultivate a habit of always encouraging ourselves, telling ourselves positive thoughts, and being our own cheerleader.

May 16

"You may not control all the events that happen to you, but you can decide not to be reduced by them."

— Maya Angelou

We get to choose how the events that happen in our lives affect us. Once we make a firm decision, we empower ourselves to have more agency over our own lives. By making these decision and empowering ourselves, we almost always feel a huge sense of relief. Even in less-than-ideal situations, we have more peace and confidence to deal with the situation, regardless of how difficult it may seem at first.

May 17

"The way to build a complex system that works is to build it from very simple systems that work."

— Kevin Kelly

Simplicity is part art and part science. As humans, we have a tendency to make things much more complex than they often need to be. By focusing on simplicity and effectiveness at a very basic level, we are then able to grow that simple system, and expand it as necessary. It is not easy, but it is worthwhile, and the effort will no doubt be rewarded with less frustration, saved time, and better outcomes.

May 18

"It is during our darkest moments that we must focus to see the light."

— Aristotle

The hard times shape and define us. Those times forge our character and help others see what we're made of. More importantly, we get to see what we are capable of and how much better we did at dealing with the difficulties than we thought we might. What are some of your most difficult challenges? What did you learn about yourself in the process of overcoming those challenges? How can you help others who are facing similar challenges?

May 19

"Once you free yourself from the need for perfect acceptance, it's a lot easier to launch work that matters."

— Seth Godin

It's good to want to do a good job. We can take it to extremes, though. If we shoot for perfection, it seems like a great idea because we want to hold ourselves to a higher standard. But, it can become counterproductive. Perfectionism is incredibly inefficient. We know that perfection is unattainable. Trying to get it perfect may take five hours, whereas getting it just good enough takes only one hour. So, when we free ourselves from trying to be perfect and permit ourselves to have some imperfections along the way, we have more time left over for the things that matter most in our lives. Are you trying to be too perfect? If you could reduce the time it takes to be perfect, what would you do with the time saved?

May 20

"A worthy goal for a year is to learn enough about a subject so that you can't believe how ignorant you were a year earlier."

— Kevin Kelly

We should all make it a goal to learn something new each day. It doesn't really matter what; what matters most is that we learned something that we didn't know before and that we move forward and connect the dots with past learning. This combination of experiences and new learning bills new pathways for future learning.

———•●•———

May 21

"For every fact there is an infinity of hypotheses."

— Robert Pirsig

There are so many possibilities that we don't usually pay attention to. If we try to imagine the facts of the future, what are the opportunities that may be available that we just don't spend enough time trying to think about? What types of great things are possible if you open your mind?

———•●•———

May 22

"Learning is not done to you, it is something you choose to do."

— Seth Godin

Is it the learner's responsibility to learn? Or, is it the teacher's responsibility to teach? Perhaps it is a mix of both. When we learn new things, magic happens, and we have the opportunity to share that new knowledge with others at some point in the future. In that way, learning is a gift that you can give over and over again.

May 23

"The Golden Rule will never fail you. It is the foundation of all other virtues."

— Kevin Kelly

What if everyone in the world was kind to each other?

May 24

"No pessimist ever discovered the secrets of the stars, or sailed to an uncharted land, or opened a new heaven to the human spirit."

— Helen Keller

Perhaps pessimists don't even know that they are pessimists. Maybe they don't know that there is another way, or they have made a choice thinking that that is the only choice that is available to them. They may even call themselves realists and vehemently point out that the world is what it is, and they have reasons for all their negativity. Good for them. We have the opportunity to make different choices. Which choice will you make today?

May 25

"Things turn out best for the people who make the best of the way things turn out."

— John Wooden

We can all learn to do a better job of making the best out of a given situation. If we get something unexpected, let's not waste time being discouraged. How can we use this to our advantage and make even more progress? When we adapt quickly and move forward with optimism and determination, we are doing something truly remarkable.

May 26

"The way you look at life can determine your success. As they say, look on the bright side. Have an optimistic attitude."

— Catherine Pulsifer

Since it's a choice, why would we ever choose anything less than the ideal of being positive, seeing the bright side of things, and being excited?

May 27

"Bad ideas, however sacred, cannot survive the company of good ones forever."

— Sam Harris

Ideas are powerful. We all probably agree that we should avoid bad ideas, but we may have great division in judging what is a good idea and what is not. What are your good ideas? Are you sure those are good? How do you know? Why do you feel that way?

May 28

"A problem is a chance for you to do your best."

— Duke Ellington

Are we really doing our very best each day? What if we could do better?

May 29

"You are never too old to set another goal or to dream a new dream."

— C.S. Lewis

When we stop dreaming, we're in real trouble. We should enjoy the present, but part of that is dreaming about what may be possible. There is great joy in following our dreams and accomplishing goals that we've set for ourselves. Often, the journey is more enjoyable than the actual realization of the dream or the accomplishment of the goal. We need to set new goals, dream new dreams, and act as if nothing can stop us. We can do anything!

May 30

"When you have a dream, you've got to grab it and never let go."

— Carol Burnett

In order to accomplish our dreams, we must first be willing to dream. Then we must believe that we can accomplish our dreams. We must act on them, move forward, resist the resistance, and push forward now and always. When we do these things, we can all accomplish our dreams and have a fantastic time along the way. What are your dreams? What's holding you back? Are the things holding you back are just figment of your imagination, or are they real? How can you take one step forward today?

May 31

"Believe you can and you're halfway there."

— Theodore Roosevelt

Our beliefs are very powerful things. We should always remember to believe in ourselves, and believe in others. There are plenty of critics out there, or those who won't believe in us or in others. It's not for them. They don't matter. They simply don't count. Who cares about what they think. We won't let their thoughts affect our forward progress.

June

June is roughly halfway through the year. We're at the halfway mark. Isn't it funny how quickly it seems to have passed?

How did your Q2 end? What are the most fun memories from the first half of the year? Have you taken the opportunity to celebrate your accomplishments? What are some areas you may be struggling with? Who might be able to help, if you ask?

———•●•———

June 1

"If I really want to improve my situation, I can work on the one thing over which I have control - myself."

— Stephen Covey

Self-control is and self-discipline is easy to write about, but hard to accomplish for most of us. This discipline though is instrumental to achievement.

June 2

"**The greatest day in your life and mine is when we take total responsibility for our attitudes. That's the day we truly grow up.**"

— John C. Maxwell

It never ceases to amaze me how few people willingly accept responsibility. Too often, my observation is that others play the blame game and make excuses for their shortcomings. While this is a natural self-defense mechanism, the real harm is that it robs the person of the pain required to get out of their cycle of dysfunction and move upward to the next level. That is a terrible waste of talent and potential.

June 3

"**You will never change your life until you change something you do daily. The secret of your success is found in your daily routine.**"

— Darren Hardy

There is profound wisdom in the idea that having a routine is important. It seems counterintuitive to many of us, but the more routine we keep the routine things, the more opportunity we have for thinking about the opportunities and capitalizing on them. Being able to think about and see opportunities for what they are, is key to our future growth and success.

———•●•———

June 4

"Preventing misunderstandings is far better than dealing with the consequences of them."

— Greg Barton

Whenever we have a misunderstanding, it takes a lot of time to work through all of it and try to get back to a point where we have a common ground. Doesn't it make more sense to focus on prevention than on a response? Is it possible that by communicating more clearly, and more articulately that we might be able to prevent misunderstandings in the first place?

———•●•———

June 5

"We must build dikes of courage to hold back the flood of fear."

— Martin Luther King Jr.

Fear is a natural emotion. If we push back the fear and boldly charge forward, almost anything is possible. It isn't easy, but it is worthwhile. Great people have been doing it for centuries.

June 6

"Plans are only good intentions unless they immediately degenerate into hard work."

— Peter Drucker

Taking action on our goals is really important. By immediately acting on our goals and having the commitment to continually work on them, we can get a lot accomplished. Planning is important, but planning alone without execution isn't very useful. When we can execute effectively and apply persistence and continual effort, we can achieve almost anything within our imagination.

June 7

"Fear is not real. It's an illusion, a phenomenon that resides entirely within your own brain."

— Darren Hardy

What if we were to unlearn fear, or learn how to embrace it and push forward in the face of fear. How much would our lives be transformed in the process? What fears are you facing today? What if that fear didn't exist and you did the thing you're thinking of... How would that make you feel? What if our fear is unfounded? What if it is possible for the thing we fear to happen, but it is highly unlikely?

June 8

"Don't shortchange yourself when it comes to investing in your own better future."

— Jim Rohn

There are no shortcuts in life for anyone craving for success. If we want the best that life has to offer, we have to be willing to do all the good, bad, and ugly things that will get us to where we want to be. So, shortchanging is not an option. Thrive for success. For example, education is essential. There is a common saying that if you think education is expensive, try ignorance. This shows that every penny you spend on your education is never wasted.

June 9

"Be a yardstick of quality. Some people aren't used to an environment where excellence is expected."

— Steve Jobs

Most of us can spot the issues that affect the quality of what we deliver. But what do we do about it? Do we work each day to improve? How about working to be the best? What areas in your work and life could use a renewed focus on quality? What areas could paying a little more attention to detail payoff for you?

June 10

"You will regret many things in life, but you will never regret being too kind or too fair."

— Brian Tracy

We all probably have memories when we haven't lived up to our own goals of kindness and fairness. We can all be kind to others. It doesn't cost anything. In an age where doing good things is often unnoticed, we must remember that being kind to others and trying to be fair are very noble, worthwhile goals. When we do these things, it is an investment in good energy in the present. What will you do to be more kind and fair today and this week?

June 11

"Optimism, positivity and faith create the foundation from which success can be built."

— Sharon Lechter

Without a strong foundation, any building will fail. Without a strong foundation in character and our beliefs, we as people can fail. What type of foundation have you built for yourself? How can we improve the foundation that our lives are built on? What would be possible if we improved our foundation and made it better and stronger than before?

June 12

"It is not enough to do your best; you must know what to do, and then do your best."

— Dr. W. Edwards Deming

A lot of people do things without thinking them through. Sadly, most people have a herd mentality in solving different problems. Well, this does not have to be the case. When we have a goal, we must sit and critically reflect on it. If not, we will be walking in the dark as many people do. Let us seek to understand our goals first, then work hard towards achieving them.

June 13

"Great businesses are not built by extraordinary people but by ordinary people doing extraordinary things."

— Michael Gerber

Every one of us is unique and extraordinary in our own intriguing ways. It is tempting to think that successful people are more amazing than we are or blessed with better qualities than we are, but this is not so. We are all the same, in that we have something special in us. The difference is what we do to with what we have to get us to where we want. People like

Mark Zuckerberg, Bill Gates, and Jack Ma are ordinary people. The only difference is that they dared to believe in their dreams and pursue them.

June 14

"I forgive all personal weaknesses except egomania and pretension."

— Herb Kelleher

Every one of us has weaknesses. We must accept everyone as they are, including their shortcomings. However, we must protect ourselves from people who keep letting us down or lowering our spirits. If you cannot trust someone, it is best to stay clear of them to protect yourself. Let us not let anyone pull us down. People can be very manipulative and have evil intentions towards you, even if you have not wronged them. Unfortunately, evil knows no family ties or friendship bonds because even a friend or a relative can betray you. Stay alert.

June 15

"The cost of being wrong is less than the cost of doing nothing."

— Seth Godin

It is best to try something and fail than to wonder later how trying it would have been. Regret is worse than failure. Do not let go of an idea that you would want to try. Take chances, and do not be discouraged by the thoughts of a misstep as it is only the start of something promising. There are no results from doing nothing. Try it. If you fail, at least there will be a lesson learned.

———•●•———

June 16

"A slip of the foot you may soon recover, but a slip of the tongue you may never get over."

— Benjamin Franklin

"Loose tongues sink ships." There are times when conflicts may cause us to say the most hurtful words with little regard to how it will affect who it was directed. The surge of emotions at such times influence us in significant ways and can result negatively. We must, therefore, be careful and watch our words at all times. Let us not forget that we are accountable for everything we do or say.

June 17

"There are no constraints on the human mind, no walls around the human spirit, no barriers to our progress except those we ourselves erect."

— Ronald Reagan

We have so much potential. More than our minds could grasp. More often than not, we create our demons and limitations. Sometimes life can cause us to view ourselves from a negative perspective. If we choose to ignore the negative voices in our heads and focus on our strengths, we will conquer all barriers and achieve our goals.

June 18

"The faster you leave your comfort zone, the faster you'll see growth."

— Marie Forleo

When was the last time you challenged yourself? What have you done in the last 30 days to step outside your comfort zone? What will you choose to do today and this week to grow. What is possible if you do? Think it through, you might be surprised by your results.

June 19

"Life is not measured by the number of breaths we take, but by the moments that take our breath away."

— Maya Angelou

Life is beautiful and precious. It is not easy. It never has been. But it is always worthwhile. What moments leave you breathless? What inspires you? What gives you a sense of awe, wonder, and amazement?

June 20

"The only factor becoming scarce in a world of abundance is human attention."

— Kevin Kelly

The human attention span is decreasing as time passes. We have less of an attention span than ever before. There are so many distractions and such little focus, our minds are always bouncing from thing to thing with less time than ever before to focus on a single task, a single idea. By eliminating distractions and focusing on whatever is most important to get done today, we instantly put ourselves miles ahead of our competitors who lack the self-discipline. The results that we can achieve through focused effort are beyond our imaginations when we have the next <ding> stealing our attention and the quality work that would be possible in the absence of it.

June 21

"The only impossible journey is the one you never begin."

— Tony Robbins

Almost anything is possible. For sure, it won't be easy. There will be frustrations and setbacks along the way. But if we move forward, repeatedly, we can get closer this week than we were last week. Just imagine how much closer we will be next week, if we're willing to give it our absolute best effort.

June 22

"Any question that's difficult to answer deserves more thought."

— Seth Godin

What are some of the most difficult questions you are facing at the moment? Like never before in human history, the internet has made answers to many questions instantly available. Those answers may not be specific to your situation, but they are a fantastic starting point.

If you have difficulty answering a question, get really curious. Look up the answer online. Conduct an experiment to see if your answer is correct. You can draw from your own perspective and seek others' perspectives for insight.

If you get really good at asking difficult questions and conducting experiments to learn, your life will be richer for having done so.

June 23

"Acquiring things will rarely bring you deep satisfaction. But acquiring experiences will."

— Kevin Kelly

Things do not make us happy; experiences can, if we choose the right experiences and can be fully and completely present to enjoy them.

June 24

"The real cycle you're working on is a cycle called yourself."

— Robert Pirsig

Almost everything in the outside world starts by understanding what's going on in hours on minds. What journey are you on in your own mind?

June 25

"When your art fails, make better art."

— Seth Godin

Is there any such thing as failure? When we get right down to it, every step along the way is required. Success doesn't come easy for anyone. It requires patience, persistence, and learning from our mistakes. Embrace those and see what is possible in your future.

June 26

"Optimism is the faith that leads to achievement. Nothing can be done without hope and confidence."

— Helen Keller

So many people view the world in a less optimistic way than would best serve them. Optimum is a choice. It is a choice that we make each day, often many times during each day. In a constantly changing world and often changing at a faster pace than ever before in human history, we would be best served to remain optimistic and embrace the future of what is possible. Anything is possible if we believe that it is.

June 27

"What I've really learned over time is that optimism is a very, very important part of leadership."

— Bob Iger

Pessimistic people should never be in positions of management or leadership. Unfortunately, they sometimes are. When they are, it makes things miserable for everyone around them. Leadership isn't a popularity contest, nor is it something that should be available to someone who cannot remain optimistic.

June 28

"How wonderful it is that nobody need wait a single moment before starting to improve the world."

— Anne Frank

We all have permission to make the world better. What will we do today to improve?

June 29

"People often regret the things they cared about. Their attention was bound up in petty concerns when life was normal."

— Sam Harris

What we care about and where we place our attention and focus are important. In a world with seemingly endless distractions, it is more important than ever before to make smart decisions when we're deciding what we care about and what we focus on. Our focus is one of our most precious resources and it seems harder than ever to be disciplined and focused. What are you focusing on? What should you be focusing on? What would be possible if you shifted your focus to something else? How will it feel when you do?

June 30

"Life has no limitations, except the ones you make."

— Les Brown

What would life be like if we didn't create our own barriers? What barriers are we unintentionally setting for ourselves without even knowing it?

July

July is a fantastic month. In July, we celebrate Independence Day in the United States, the birth of our nation. We are a young nation and we have made some mistakes along the way. But we've also changed the world as a result of the idea of freedom.

Are you independent? To what degree do you remain dependent on others? How could that situation possibly change? Does it seem hopeless, likely, or certain? If you were to think differently, are there possibilities to improve the situation that you might be overlooking? Ask yourself, "what if" a lot and see if you might be able to see some opportunities.

July 1

"Start with the end in mind."

— Stephen Covey

I often think of this as backwards thinking. Think about what the end goal, objective, or mission to be accomplished. What is the end state? What does it look like? How will we know when we have succeeded? Once we are clear on this, being able to work backwards and set milestones for achievement is much easier. All too often, I see people kicking the can down the road with no early idea what it is they're trying to accomplish. The end result in that game is wasted time, energy, lost opportunities, and less effectiveness than what is possible.

July 2

"Life is 10% what happens to me and 90% of how I react to it."

— John C. Maxwell

Always good to remember that how we react or respond to a situation is a choice we make. Sometimes it happens very quickly, almost like our brains are on autopilot. This situation still happens to me far more frequently than I would like to admit. Each time it does, I try to take a moment to reflect on the situation. Then, I ask myself what I could have done differently. Then, I resolve to myself that the next time that happens, here's what I'm going to do instead. This process serves as a pre-planned response that I find incredibly useful in a continually changing world. For me, this is simple, fast, and effective! This method helps me tremendously.

July 3

"Don't wish it were easier; wish you were better."

— Darren Hardy

Striving for continual improvement is an easy, but it is worthwhile. I'm getting better every day, better every week, every month, and every year that passes, we transform ourselves into a better version. By wishing we were better, and focusing on that and applying the principles contained in this book, we can all grow and improve.

———•●•———

July 4

"Never get so close to your position that when your position goes, your ego goes with it."

— Colin Powell

We will all be served well if we remember to check our ego at the door, remain humble, work hard, do a good job, and treat others with kindness and respect.

———•●•———

July 5

"When a subject becomes totally obsolete we make it a required course."

— Peter Drucker

Traditional academic subjects are important. It's important to have a good foundation. Today though, the world operates at a faster pace than ever before. What kind of learning would benefit us? What investment will you make this year in your own personal growth and development?

July 6

"Don't follow your dreams. Chase them down with aggressive pursuit."

— Darren Hardy

The journey of going after what we want brings us to life. What are your dreams? When was the last time you sat down and wrote down what you're dreaming of? How would you feel if you accomplished your dreams? If you're waiting before working on them, why? What is holding you back?

July 7

"We must develop and maintain the capacity to forgive. He who is devoid of the power to forgive is devoid of the power to love. There is some good in the worst of us and some evil in the best of us. When we discover this, we are less prone to hate our enemies."

— Martin Luther King Jr.

Carrying around hatred and negative energy comes at a terrible cost. When we are able to learn, forgive, and shift our focus to more positive things, it serves us much better than continuing to remember things that don't serve us. We are our thoughts, actions, and behaviors. Taking a proactive role in deciding what serves us best, rather than being subject to the default feeling, is a fantastic way to make our lives better.

July 8

"Don't wish it was easier, wish you were better. Don't wish for less problems, wish for more skills. Don't wish for less challenges, wish for more wisdom."

— Jim Rohn

Sometimes life can get us into an unpleasant situation that may cause us to wish things were more comfortable. But, we can change all of these by changing our perspectives on the challenges we face. Instead of whining about a situation, we could choose to see what we can learn from it and how it can make us better. The reality of life is that life is not easy, and everyone, no matter how rich they are, have their own set of problems to deal with. There is a quote that says, "The only time you will not have problems is when you die." So learn to solve them rather than run away from them.

July 9

"My favorite things in life don't cost any money. It's really clear that the most precious resource we all have is time."

— Steve Jobs

What ways are we spending our time less wisely than we should be doing? What will we do about it? If time is really like currency, and I believe it is, why don't we regularly act with greater degrees of intention and focus on how to use this gift better? What ways will you modify your routine, to make better use of your time this week?

July 10

"The key to good decision making is not knowledge. It is understanding. We are swimming in the former. We are desperately lacking in the latter."

— Malcolm Gladwell

There are a lot of information around us. Google has even made it easier to acquire information on anything we want. But, this information is useless if we do not understand it and put it to good use. With a good understanding of things, we are proof of bad decisions that may cost us a lot. Seek to understand.

July 11

"All great achievements are the result of sustained focus over time - all of them."

— Gary Keller

Focus is more important than ever. It always has been. But, today, distraction is rampant in society and media. The progress that is possible with the right amount of focus and determination cannot be overstated.

July 12

"If you let your emotions get high, your bargaining power will be low. Make sure you don't negotiate from a position of need when making a deal."

— Sharon Lechter

Emotions are natural to all human beings. However, we must be careful about how it influences us in our daily lives, particularly in business. We may come across instances in our careers that may cause our emotions to hit the ceiling. At such times, we must practice self-control to ensure that you maintain peace between you and the other party. Hard, but possible.

July 13

"The big problems are where people don't realise they have one in the first place."

— Dr. W. Edwards Deming

There is nothing as hard as trying to help someone who does not see that they needed help. Some of us have had instances when our loved ones get into trouble yet do not realize that they have a problem. It can be tough. These situations require a lot of patience and wisdom to handle. But it is still possible to find solutions to the issues.

July 14

"You have everything you need to build something far bigger than yourself."

— Seth Godin

"Use what you have" This is a phrase that most of us have probably heard. Sometimes we may be tempted to think that the solutions to our problems are far from reach. However, it may surprise you to realize that you already have what it takes. When we start with what we have, we shall grow and gradually acquire what we need to achieve our goals.

July 15

"Tell me and I forget. Teach me and I remember. Involve me and I learn."

— Benjamin Franklin

To effectively teach a skill, it is best to involve the mentee in the activities we do. Involvement creates a mental familiarity with the lesson taught. When we choose to be involved in what we are learning, we will understand it better and faster than someone who only knows the concept.

July 16

"There are no great limits to growth because there are no limits of human intelligence, imagination, and wonder."

— Ronald Reagan

Whatever hurdle we go through, we can always find a way out. We have the intelligence and ability to have different ideas, and build on them. Imagination and possibilities are our limitless resources.

July 17

"I win or I learn, but I never lose."

— Marie Forleo

We only lose when we don't try. Almost anything is possible if we try enough and continue pivoting and learning along the way. Most ordinary humans give up far too easily. Don't give up. Try more. Learn more. Do more and get more. We can do anything we want to do if we're willing to learn and keep trying until we get the outcome we're after.

July 18

"Success is liking yourself, liking what you do, and liking how you do it."

— Maya Angelou

What are the voices inside our minds saying to us? What are our thoughts? How do they make us feel? Are they positive and uplifting? Do they inspire us? Or do they make us feel bad about ourselves? Do they hold us back because we feel as though we aren't good enough, smart enough, or capable enough? The good news is that we're already good enough, smart enough, and capable enough to do amazing things. What amazing thing will you do this year?

July 19

"The only organization capable of unprejudiced growth, or unguided learning, is a network. All other topologies limit what can happen."

— Kevin Kelly

Who makes up our network? Are they helping us grow? Who do we need to add to our network to help us expand our thinking and strengthen our existing strengths? Who will help support us in the areas that we're less strong in than we need to be? Who will we add to our networks today, this week, this month, and this year that, if we were looking backwards in time five years from now, would make the most profound difference?

July 20

"It's all about finding the calm in the chaos."

— Donna Karan

Chaos isn't desired, but it happens. What will you do when it rears its ugly head? Will you gripe and complain? Or, will you stay calm and focus on the solution? Will you be amused by it and let others around you suffer? Or will you pitch in and do your part? Will you be selfish, or will you be generous and help create a new future amidst the uncertainty?

July 21

"You only live once, but if you do it right, once is enough."

— Mae West

We all have the opportunity to make the best life for ourselves. We need to remember to pause long enough to look back and reflect on things. Are we living the best life possible? What changes do we need to make to live an even better life this time next year than we're living today?

July 22

"Quality tends to fan out like waves."

— Robert Pirsig

We should remember that quality dissipates the further it goes from the source. To maintain good quality, we have to be intentional. It requires hard work and effort. Systems, processes, checks, and balances are helpful. Ultimately though, quality often comes down to how much someone cares. We have to have faith in the fact that we can make a difference and improve quality as long as we care and put forth the right amount of energy, focus, and determination.

July 23

"**You can't have good ideas unless you're willing to generate a lot of bad ones.**"

— Seth Godin

We all have good and bad ideas. We all have within us the capacity to do good things or to do bad things. Sometimes, people do horrible things. But the world is filled with examples of goodness, and peoples' good works. We try to succeed, and often, we make mistakes. Experiments fail. Not all decisions are good ones. The important thing is that we learn from them as we go and move forward in life. If we continue to keep going, we can do almost anything.

July 24

"**Anything real begins with the fiction of what could be. Imagination is therefore the most potent force in the universe, and a skill you can get better at. It's the one skill in life that benefits from ignoring what everyone else knows.**"

— Kevin Kelly

As adults, I believe that we lose focus on the power of imagination. Almost anything that we imagined can come true if we are willing to put the right amount of energy and dedication into it. This is why it is essential to take time and let your mind wander, to drift off and think about things—daydreaming, envisioning what could be possible. When is the last time you spent 10 minutes daydreaming? What if we scheduled opportunities to daydream on our calendar? Doing a daily practice of this may yield positive results beyond what we presently think is possible.

July 25

"The real purpose of the scientific method is to make sure nature hasn't misled you into thinking you know something you actually don't know."

— Robert Pirsig

Unless we are educated or work in a scientific field, most of us as adults get away from the scientific method. There is a lot to be learned about the scientific method and what results may be possible if we use it. By being more deliberate, more methodical, and experimenting, we have the ability to learn and grow in ways that others are willing to do.

July 26

"Optimism is essential to achievement and it is also the foundation of courage and true progress."

— Nicholas M. Butler

We must boldly charge forward, knowing that we will succeed if we have the right attitude and just keep persisting despite all the obstacles we may encounter along the way. We can and we will, but only if we decide that we will.

July 27

"I have never had to face anything that could overwhelm the native optimism and stubborn perseverance I was blessed with."

— Justice Sonia Sotomayor

Don't let the pessimists wear you down. They will if you let them. You're smarter than that, and you know that you'll succeed where they will be stuck. Don't blame them, though. They just don't see the world differently, in a more optimistic way that comes effortlessly to you and me.

July 28

"If you're not making someone else's
life better, then you're wasting your
time. Your life will become better by
making other lives better."

— Will Smith

We can all do something. Remember, all the little things add up to big things too. Something as simple as a random act of kindness counts in ways we may not be able to truly understand. What if we each make an effort to make three people's lives better today?

July 29

"The reality of your life is now."

— Sam Harris

When we realize that now is the most important thing we're dealing with, it is easier to shift our attention to the present and become fully engaged. Planning for the future is important, but being fully present — right now — is where we should spend most of our time. We should reflect on the past, plan for the future, but live in the now. What are some ways you can become more present?

July 30

"Positive thoughts lead to positive results."

— Maria V. Snyder

Negative thoughts make us feel bad and waste energy. Positive thoughts help us feel better and are an investment in the future. Which makes the most sense to you? Who can you help influence to be slightly more positive today? What might they achieve if they do? How can you help facilitate this?

July 31

"Keep your face to the sunshine and you cannot see a shadow."

— Helen Keller

When we remind ourselves each day that we have the ability to influence the future by simply making better choices, we bring to life a better world with more choices and better things. We have the power of choice. We need to remember that each day, and focus on making sure that we align ourselves with what's possible.

August

August is hot, hot, hot in the Southern United States. It is the month that includes International Youth Day. We're in the middle of Q3 and time seems to be passing by faster than it did last year. Or does it?

Are you on track to accomplish all the things you'd like by the end of the year? How are the adjustments that you've made thus far working out? Are you succeeding or struggling? What will you do about it? Who can help offer support to you and assure you succeed?

August 1

"Two people can see the same thing, disagree, and yet both be right. It's not logical; it's psychological."

— Stephen Covey

I spent a great majority of my life wondering why people always seemed to act illogically. Finally, with age and insight I learned that emotions drive people's decisions much more frequently than logic does. Many have difficulties separating their emotion from logic. This is a terribly expensive mistake that most of us should have outgrown by our mid-twenties.

August 2

"If we are growing we are always going to be outside our comfort zone."

— John C. Maxwell

Since staying outside our comfort zone is best for our growth, wouldn't it make the most sense if we intentionally plan to do things that make us uncomfortable it we are to get used to it and to thrive in that situation? By pushing ourselves, growth and development are quite possible. Anything is possible that we can envision for our future.

August 3

"You alone are responsible for what you do, don't do, or how you respond to what's done to you."

— Darren Hardy

Leaders accept responsibility. Children blame others. If we want to be a better leader or get a promotion or pay raise, we should seek and accept greater responsibility and stop playing the blame game. Whether it is internal or external, the blame game only seeks to further distract us from the important work that we were meant to do.

August 4

"Control enthusiasm in the face of victories, large or small."

— Colin Powell

Play it cool. It normally works out better. It may not feel as good initially, but the end result is what we're after and others will remember our actions.

August 5

"Efficiency is doing better what is already being done."

— Peter Drucker

All other things being equal, getting better, is better than doing nothing. Sometimes we need to also look at effectiveness, because being efficient at things that aren't effective isn't the best use of our energy. What can we do to become more efficient today? Will that be sufficient, or should we examine our level of effectiveness instead?

August 6

"What controls your attention, controls your life."

— Darren Hardy

We should remember to focus on what we want, not what we don't. When we eliminate distractions, we will have plenty of time for the things that are most important to us.

August 7

"Rarely do we find men who willingly engage in hard, solid thinking. There is an almost universal quest for easy answers and half-baked solutions. Nothing pains some people more than having to think."

— Martin Luther King Jr.

What do you think is very important to our future? Our thoughts determine what we feel and how we see the world. Our thoughts determine what we say to others. Our thoughts determine what we choose to do and choose not to do. Our thoughts lead to feelings, which lead to behaviors and actions, which leads to outcomes. What outcomes are we most proud of? What are some of the thoughts that likely led to that outcome? What are some areas where we're falling short? What thoughts must be changed in order to move the needle in that area?

August 8

"Some people dream of success, while others wake up and work hard at it."

— Napoleon Hill

Dreaming is important and almost required for achievement. But, having a dream or vision without following it with action, commitment, persistence, and determination won't get us much closer to making that dream a reality. What are your dreams? What visions do you have for the future? What are you doing to make your reality match that vision?

August 9

"The big challenge is to become all that you have the possibility of becoming. You cannot believe what it does to the human spirit to maximize your human potential and stretch yourself to the limit."

— Jim Rohn

Each of us is born with an innate potential to grow in different areas of life. We have more potential to do things than we could ever imagine. If we live through life with this in mind, we can achieve everything we set our minds on. This mentality will create a victor's attitude in us, motivating us more towards our goals.

***

August 10

"Creativity is just connecting things."

— Steve Jobs

There are a lot of creative people in our society. It was not only meant for the artists but everyone. We all have the potential to be creative in different life situations. We cannot afford to sit around through hard times and wait for the hardships to pass. We must be innovative and come up with ways to make things easier. It is surprising how fun it could be.

***

August 11

"Those three things — autonomy, complexity, and a connection between effort and reward — are, most people will agree, the three qualities that work has to have if it is to be satisfying."

— Malcolm Gladwell

Everyone loves rewards. Clearly, it's great when we are rewarded externally, but, let's not forget about the internal reward that we get when we do a job particularly well. Taking pride in our work and the satisfaction that we get from doing a job exceptionally well is fantastic. That feeling cannot be bought with money. It is something that everyone should be able to feel at least a few times during each week. What projects are you near completing that will make you feel great for having done a superb job?

August 12

"The road to success is always under construction."

— Gary Keller

Making things work isn't easy. It requires thought, planning, and adjustment. It requires effort, conversations, and coordination. There's so much that goes in to success. Going from "how things have always been" into "how things should be" is never easy. It is hard work. It's sometimes messy. Often, it involves growing pains. But in the end, the efforts are worthwhile once something new and worthwhile emerges.

August 13

"We believe what we want to believe in, and once we believe something, it becomes a self-fulfilling truth."

— Seth Godin

We have our own beliefs, which generally crop up from our backgrounds, life experiences, and other factors. The things about us humans are that once we believe in something, they become an integral part of us. Whatever we believe in can become real, because the universe works in accordance with our beliefs.

August 14

"To succeed, jump as quickly at opportunities as you do at conclusions."

— Benjamin Franklin

There are very many opportunities to grow in different areas. To succeed, you need to find these opportunities so you can grow in your areas of expertise. By bouncing fast on those opportunities, we get to get a lot of ideas and connect with people in the same areas of interest. These are essential for growth and eventually, success.

August 15

"Progress not perfection is the only way to bridge the gap between your ability and your ambition."

— Marie Forleo

Progress is hard. Perfection is desired but impossible. Our best progress is made when we set goals, track our actions, celebrate our success, and reflect on what we could have done better. How can we get those with whom we work to strive to do better work, improve things that need to be improved, and empowered to make a positive difference that we all can be proud of?

August 16

"One isn't necessarily born with courage, but one is born with potential. Without courage, we cannot practice any other virtue with consistency. We can't be kind, true, merciful, generous, or honest."

— Maya Angelou

How many people have we all met that don't have the courage to be honest with themselves? What would have been possible for them had they made different choices, committed to different things, and made more meaningful contributions?

August 17

"It is easy to make a dollar but it is hard to make a difference."

— Kevin Kelly

Each of us has something unique to offer to help someone else. The only way not to make a difference is to not care. Step outside your bubble and get involved in being a part of the solution that is need, not the one that's easiest and requires minimal effort. Avoid the excuses, take responsibility, step up, and make a difference that you'll be proud of, this time next year when you're looking back and reflecting on your success.

August 18

"In calmness lies true pleasure."

— Victor Hugo

Each day, I strive to remain calm despite all the opportunities to freak the hell out. Sometimes I stumble and I don't succeed as well as I'd prefer. I try to learn from those occasions and think about what I will do the next time that situation arises.

August 19

"**Peace is not absence of conflict, it is the ability to handle conflict by peaceful means.**"

— Ronald Reagan

Conflict is inevitable. Peaceful ways is a smart choice. More people should consider using it and see what a profound impact it can have on their lives.

August 20

"**Life is a long lesson in humility.**"

— James M. Barrie

Are we doing enough to be humble? Do we accept responsibility rather than play the blame game? Are we willing to learn and grow because we're well aware — and not afraid to admit — that we don't have all the answers? Do we actively listen and try to hear and truly understand, rather than simply listening and trying to find an opportunity to respond in disagreement? Do we know that we're worth being patient, rather than trying to boast in order to make others see how good we are? Do we have the right ethical boundaries, moral values, and core values that help guide our decision-making, or do we put ourselves first because our own inflated ego demands that from us?

August 21

"Attitude is a little thing that makes a big difference."

— Winston Churchill

Attitude is everything. There is not cure for a bad attitude. There is little hope for a closed-minded person with a bad attitude.

August 22

"The more you read, the more you calm down."

— Robert Pirsig

There's something calming about reading because we get the opportunity to see things from another perspective, one that's outside of the perspective we're stuck with inside our own minds. When we read, we can relate. We can learn and grow. We can see that we are simply a part of something that is much larger than simply ourselves.

August 23

"The confusion kicks in when we become overwhelmed by all the things we can do, but can't find the time or the courage to actually commit and follow through."

— Seth Godin

Things are really difficult when you are overwhelmed. When you are confused, you can act irrationally or make highly emotional decisions that aren't the best. You can become quite impatient, rude, and even toxic. Overwhelm is a terrible state of mind.

In my observation, now more than ever in recent human history, the distractions we face are at epic levels. All these distractions take away from the work that you need to do the most. Overcoming overwhelm comes from having a clear commitment and taking persistent action. What are your most important commitments? Are your actions in alignment with those commitments?

August 24

"Don't be the best. Be the only."

— Kevin Kelly

How would it feel to be a category of one? In what areas can you become a category of one?

August 25

"In the high country of the mind one has to become adjusted to the thinner air of uncertainty..."

— Robert Pirsig

As I write this book in 2020, this is the year of the pandemic and the year of uncertainty. It seems like it has been a year of Murphy's law in real life, and the entire world as we thought we knew it, has been flipped into one we have more trouble recognizing and understanding. We do an excellent service to ourselves when we embrace uncertainty and the unknown. Rather than rejecting it and wishing it wasn't true, we should do our best to embrace it and learn to deal with the situation as it is now. It feels like a new world with much more uncertainty. That means much greater opportunities. We can choose how we think about things and decide to be grateful, and decide to move forward with an adventurous spirit.

August 26

"Optimism refuses to believe that the road ends without options."

— Robert Schuller

There are more opportunities in the world than can be capitalized on. The key is to learn to spot them easily and be able to decide on the best ones to go after. There are always options. If our minds are closed, we can't see them. When we keep an open mind, the options and opportunities can more easily find us.

August 27

"Optimism can be more powerful than a battery of artillery or squadron of tanks. It can be contagious and it's necessary to being a leader."

— Gen. Rick Hillier

Optimism inspires others. Luckily, it is also contagious. Negativity is cancer to an individual or an organization. The only way to defeat negativity is positivity.

August 28

"Regardless of who wins, an election should be a time for optimism and fresh approaches."

— Gary Johnson

As I write this, we are approaching the 2020 elections. Our country has experienced many challenges in the past. One of the more difficult challenges I see is the ideology that our country is facing. I don't recall a time when our nation has been more divided along a line between the political parties. We need to remember that we are one nation, that we are all in this together, and move forward knowing that whoever holds the office is, to some degree, irrelevant. We all have the power to choose optimism and succeed, despite any challenges that may arise. Why, then, do so many people get so distracted with politics? We can think of different thoughts that lead to other actions that will inevitably yield different results. We always get better outcomes when we make wise choices.

August 29

"My dear friend, clear your mind of can't."

— Samuel Johnson

I'm always inspired by other "can do" people who push forward despite obstacles and setbacks. We must decide, be committed, and take the necessary actions. When we are committed and persistent, almost anything is possible.

———•●•———

August 30

"Nothing is impossible. The word itself says "I'm possible!""

— Audrey Hepburn

Anything is possible with the right amount of optimism and effort. Sure, there are details to be worked out. There will be skeptics and naysayers. There always are. Don't listen to them. They don't see what is possible because they're too stuck in the muck to see what great things can be done. That's not your problem; it's theirs. Choose the possible. It will become so.

———•●•———

August 31

"Never bend your head. Always hold it high. Look the world straight in the eye."

— Helen Keller

Be proud and confident. Only you can be you. We must face the challenges head-on and embrace the uncertainty that each day holds.

September

September is famous for Labor Day and is associated with the end of summer.

How has your summer been? Have you taken time for yourself? Have you taken the chance to get some downtime and refresh your outlook? If not, when will you schedule it? Put it on your calendar. Take care of yourself so you can finish the year with confidence and strength.

———•●•———

September 1

"Everything is Figureoutable."

— Marie Forleo

Similar to the idea that where there is a will, there is a way. If it was easy to get done or figure out, someone else would have done it already. Think on it. Get curious. Consider alternatives. Ask yourself "What if" a lot. Future you, will thank you for it.

———•●•———

September 2

"You have to decide what your highest priorities are and have the courage— pleasantly, smilingly, nonapologetically, to say "No" to other

things. And the way you do that is by having a bigger "Yes" burning inside. The enemy of the "best" is often the "good.""

— Stephen Covey

Saying "No" has never been easy for me. I have always believed in being helpful to others and do far more than expected. Saying no to someone who asks for something is not easy, yet it makes sense that if we have a bigger, more important priority to say "Yes" to, then saying no should be easier.

~—•●•—~

September 3

"Learn to say "No" to the good so you can say "Yes" to the best."

— John C. Maxwell

What will you say "Yes" to this week? What will you say "No" to? Why? If we constantly focus on the best and most important opportunities, improvement will naturally follow. Only by saying "Yes" to more important things and "No" to lesser important things can we truly grow and develop into the authentic best version of ourselves.

September 4

"In essence, you make your choices, and then your choices make you."

— Darren Hardy

Choices have consequences, both bad and good. As we make better and better choices, things naturally improve. We, of course, are the beneficiary of those improvements in various ways. Act with belief, make better choices, and see what happens after a year.

September 5

"There is no end to the good you can do if you don't care who gets the credit."

— Colin Powell

Most of us have worked with people who need all the credit. There are a great many who need to be recognized, rewarded, and praised regularly for their efforts. Let them get the credit. Keep doing good stuff no matter what. You'll always outpace them if you do.

September 6

"Every man must decide whether he will walk in the light of creative altruism or in the darkness of destructive selfishness."

— Martin Luther King Jr.

There are great benefits from being a we person instead of a me person. Being generally concerned about the needs of others is an important part of an effective leadership. When others are selfish or concerned mostly about themselves or their own individual needs, they reduce what is possible. What are some of the areas you may be able to inspire others to be more selfless, and focus on others rather than themselves?

September 7

"It is literally true that you can succeed best and quickest by helping others succeed."

— Napoleon Hill

Helping others is both gratifying and rewarding. How can we make a bigger impact and help others in a bigger way? What are three things you will do this week to make a bigger impact?

September 8

"Time is the scarcest resource and unless it is managed nothing else can be managed."

— Peter Drucker

We all recognize that it's important to manage our time. We should also recognize how difficult it can be to change our patterns related to time management. Do you think you're good at estimating how long it will take you to get something accomplished? What about if we conducted an experiment to see how good we really are at estimating the length of time needed to do something, managing our time as we are doing it, and getting things done in the time we thought was possible? What will the result be? What will we do with the knowledge we gain from conducting the experiment?

September 9

"Character is a quality that embodies many important traits, such as integrity, courage, perseverance, confidence and wisdom. Unlike your fingerprints that you are born with and

can't change, character is something that you create within yourself and must take responsibility for changing."

— Jim Rohn

We all have to decide what we stand for, what we believe in, and who we will be. When we know these things clearly and with certainty, it's much easier to observe situations where there are things that are against our character. What will we do when this occurs? Through life, there will be many tests. How will we respond?

September 10

"Don't let the noise of others' opinions drown out your own inner voice."

— Steve Jobs

Everyone has an opinion. Most people want to share those with you. Almost everyone feels like their opinion is right. It never ceases to amaze me. Very few people have the capability and intent to remain unbiased, neutral, and listen to try to understand someone else's point of view. It is part art, part science. It isn't easy, but it is necessary. Well it is good to be able to take other people's opinions into account, it is also important to know what you stand for, what you believe in, and be able to follow through with your vision of the future and what you plan to create. Without question, other people won't always understand. There will be resistance. There will be people who do not like it. There will be people who do not understand it. There will be those who don't care about you or what you're trying to do. Do it anyway, because it is the right thing to do. Because they can't understand it there's no reason not to continue and do excellent work.

September 11

"A lot of what is most beautiful about the world arises from struggle."

— Malcolm Gladwell

Most of the things that inspire us were birthed at unpleasant times. Most of the people we admire have had to struggle to get to where they are. This should encourage us to change our perspective about hard times and see them as moments that promote growth within us and make us stronger. How we react to a situation is what determines whether we fail or come out as conquerors.

September 12

"Success is built sequentially. It's one thing at a time."

— Gary Keller

The thing about most people — especially the youth — is that we want instant success. Development and technology have caused many to believe that success comes as fast as buying some snacks from the vending machine. Well, it would be sad to realize otherwise when it is too late. Great success takes time, disappointments, and a lot of failures. Keep working on it, and you will get there.

September 13

"Change will not come if we wait for some other person or if we wait for some other time."

— Barack Obama

If we desire to see change, we must start with the "man in the mirror." Michael Jackson made this very clear. We must be willing to be pioneers in the change that we want. Otherwise, we are not supposed to complain about anything if we cannot change it.

September 14

"Quitting is not the same as failing."

— Seth Godin

Yes, persistence is key. But, sometimes, it takes courage to call it quits. Some goals are not worth pursuing. We may get to the realization that our priorities change. In such a case, we do not have to waste any more time on the matter. We are allowed to quit and pursue other goals.

September 15

"**Without continual growth and progress, such words as improvement, achievement, and success have no meaning.**"

— Benjamin Franklin

The world is ever-evolving, and we should keep up the pace. Seeking personal growth, new wisdom, and challenging experience are what keeps us going.

September 16

"**Human beings are judging machines. The trick is to have a sense of humor about it. Don't personalize it, dwell on it, or indulge in it.**"

— Marie Forleo

If I had a penny for every judgmental, opinionated, small-minded knuckle head out there who thinks they're better, more qualified, more talented, etc. Stop the judgment. Stop the opinions. Get working on yourself and what you can do to make a positive difference. Look at yourself first and work on being the best version of yourself before you judge and criticize.

September 17

"There is a very fine line between loving life and being greedy for it."

— Maya Angelou

Greed is dangerous. Gratitude and love can conquer all.

September 18

"The proper response to a lousy idea is not to stop thinking. It is to come up with a better idea."

— Kevin Kelly

I'm most always amazed at how good other people believe themselves to be at point out someone else's shortcomings. They know it all, and are experts even though they themselves have deficiencies far greater. When we work to have better ideas and focus on solutions, then we're really doing something that counts and makes a real difference. Almost anyone can point out a problem. That's ridiculously easy. Improving it is where the excitement meets opportunity. The result will be an improvement that causes people to notice the progress.

September 19

"You should feel beautiful and you
should feel safe. What you surround
yourself with should bring you peace of
mind and peace of spirit."

— Stacy London

We should all be surrounded with the most positive and
supportive people we can find. Often, we may find that we
need to be aware of our surroundings and rebalance those who
we are around the most. Go for the positive. Go for those who
are supportive, encouraging, and kind.

September 20

"Positive anything is better than
negative nothing."

— Elbert Hubbard

If it wasn't for negative people, the positive ones might seem
like less of a joy to be around.

September 21

"We keep passing unseen through little moments of other people's lives."

— Robert Pirsig

When we're all stuck inside our own minds and our own thoughts, it's easy to overlook the impact we have on others. We can conduct a thought experiment where we consider how things might affect others, how they might feel about it, and what their needs might be. When we think of others' perspectives and try to act in a positive, productive way, then we are doing truly great work, that is sure to yield better results.

September 22

"Don't try to be the 'next'. Instead, try to be the other, the changer, the new."

— Seth Godin

What are you doing to change things? Are the changes for the better? Are you acting in the spirit of generosity, or are you offering those changes to be selfish? Are you opinionated and negative, or are you optimistic, willing, and grateful? When is the last time you did something new? What did you learn from it? What is the next new thing you plan to do?

September 23

"Don't be the smartest person in the room. Hangout with, and learn from, people smarter than yourself. Even better, find smart people who will disagree with you."

— Kevin Kelly

Who do you need to connect with to get to the next level? Make a short list of 3 to 5 people you will reach out to this week. Who knows what can come of it!

September 24

"One of the most moral acts is to create a space in which life can move forward."

— Robert Pirsig

We're constantly moving forward. Life progresses, and it doesn't delay for anyone or anything. We sometimes wish it wasn't that way, and we tend to try and resist it. We all know that resistance is useless, but we often do it anyway. What if we imagine what is possible if we were to easily overcome that resistance, such that forward progress is effortless, like the water flowing gently down a stream with no effort required?

September 25

"A pessimist sees the difficulty in every opportunity; an optimist sees the opportunity in every difficulty."

— Winston Churchill

We have to remember that others may see the world far different than we see it. How boring would the world be if we were all the same? If given a choice, will we decide that we will be pessimists or optimists? Wouldn't it make more sense to be optimistic and learn to see possibility where others only see problems?

September 26

"Self-belief, optimism, and hard work, these things don't guarantee to get any of us to the top, but they at least give us a fighting chance."

— Jason Ayres

There is much less opportunity for those with a pessimistic disposition. So much energy is spent analyzing the negative, criticizing others, trying to place blame, complaining, etc. It is a waste of human potential.

September 27

"You have to look to the future with optimism instead of negative ideas. Take the good and the bad and face it head on."

— Goldie Hawn

Anything is possible when we believe that it is possible. What if we were able to remain neutral and less emotionally invested in the things that we observe. Then, we will have the opportunity to choose our response rather than being forced to react. A positive response is always better than a default reaction. Act with intention rather than defaulting to options that won't serve us well.

September 28

"Do what is right, not what is easy nor what is popular."

— Roy T. Bennett

What's popular is often not what's truly right. Then again, what's right may depend on our perspective. What's right for one is often wrong for someone else. In situations like these, it helps to have an optimistic disposition, because if we are able to see things in a positive manner and if we take the time to consider different perspectives, we are more likely to make the decision that we will view as right when we're ten years in the future looking backward.

———————•●•——————

September 29

"Problems are not stop signs, they are guidelines."

— Robert Schuller

What if we viewed each problem as an opportunity to improve? What if we acted on those insofar as possible and made continuous improvements? What would be possible if we did this day after day, year after year, decade after decade? Be optimistic and keep moving forward.

———————•●•——————

September 30

"When everything seems to be going against you, remember that the airplane takes off against the wind, not with it."

— Henry Ford

What if we viewed everything that seems to work against us as the very thing that will help ensure our eventual success? After all, isn't that the way that it truly is?

October

October is fun because we get to look forward to the fun of Halloween.

It is also the beginning of the fourth quarter of the year. This is the beginning of the final stretch. How are you doing so far? What will your final push look like? Remember, there are several holidays between now and the end of the year, so plan accordingly. What do you need to adjust in order to have your best year? Let's finish the year with vigor.

———•●•———

October 1

"We are free to choose our actions, but we are not free to choose the consequences of these actions."

— Stephen Covey

Choices have consequences. The ability to see the potential consequence of a choice in advance is a skill that takes a little getting used to. Sometimes it's hard to see the consequences ahead of time. I believe this is why things often go astray — the law of unintended consequences.

October 2

"The greatest mistake we make is living in constant fear that we will make one."

— John C. Maxwell

We all make mistakes. We accept that. We accept the mistakes of others, so why are we so hard on ourselves? By accepting that we will make mistakes and giving ourselves permission to do so, we empower ourselves to boldly move forward. Mistakes will happen. We should try to learn from our mistakes, but not be too harsh on ourselves for making them.

October 3

"If you want to get from where you are to where you want to be, you have to start by becoming aware of the choices that lead you away from your desired destination."

— Darren Hardy

Ask yourself each day, am I moving closer to my desired end-state or farther away from it? If you appear to be moving farther away, think about why and adjust your course before you get too far along your journey. Nothing wrong with adjusting the plan along the way.

October 4

"I came to the conclusion that there is an existential moment in your life when you must decide to speak for yourself; nobody else can speak for you."

— Martin Luther King Jr.

We become stronger when we know what we believe in, and why. We each have the ability to have our own beliefs, stand for what we believe in, and assure our actions match our stated beliefs. In a world that is more distracted than ever before, knowing yourself and what you believe in — not what others have tried to persuade you to believe — is incredibly important and valuable. What are your core values? What are the principles you believe most strongly in?

October 5

"Strength and growth come only through continuous effort and struggle."

— Napoleon Hill

Everyone struggles in someway or another. Does it not make the most sense to struggle to grow, develop ourselves, and become the best versions of ourselves? Where are you on your journey of becoming the best version of yourself?

October 6

"We now accept the fact that learning is a lifelong process of keeping abreast of change. And the most pressing task is to teach people how to learn."

— Peter Drucker

Change, as we all know, is inevitable. Thus, we will always have something new to learn, no matter what stage we are in life. When we accept this, we will readily accept and be eager for the changes that occur in life. However, we must be willing to learn something from every situation we face, whether pleasant or not.

October 7

"The moment you feel the need to tightly manage someone, you've made a hiring mistake. The best people don't need to be managed. Guided, taught, led—yes. But not tightly managed."

— Jim Collins

It is not easy to trust people with your job or business. I mean, nobody knows a dream better than the dream bearer. This might cause a lot of bosses to micromanage their subordinates.

This is, however, unnecessary. Good bosses see their employees as mentees who need guidance to learn what requires to be done. Be a good boss — guide.

———•●•———

October 8

"**Never get so close to your position that when your position goes, your ego goes with it.**"

— Colin Powell

Being right all the time and being prideful of that comes at a terrible cost. Sometimes, it's better to be wrong and move forward. Leave the ego at the door and move forward.

———•●•———

October 9

"**Being the richest man in the cemetery doesn't matter to me. Going to bed at night saying we've done something wonderful… that's what matters to me.**"

— Steve Jobs

There are many wealthy people in the world with everything they could ever want in life but living dull lives. Success in life is not basing on how much money you have, but on the impact and influence that goes hand in hand, especially to the people around us. We could be rich and happy, but let us seek value in life by doing good deeds. True happiness comes by making others happy.

———•●•———

October 10

"When you know what's important, it's a lot easier to ignore what's not."

— Marie Forleo

Selective attention is one of the best skills that anyone can ever learn. We all have loads of people and things to pay attention to. If we pay attention to all of them, we may be too overwhelmed to focus on what matters.

———•●•———

October 11

"There has been one constant ... America's men and women in uniform have served with courage and resolve."

— Barack Obama

Some of the most under-appreciated people are the men and women in uniform. These people take significant risks to ensure that the streets are safe and that the law is being followed to the latter. We cannot ignore that most of them sacrifice a lot for the sake of this country. We should remember to render them courtesy and respect for a job well done.

October 12

"You can raise the bar or you can wait for others to raise it, but it's getting raised regardless."

— Seth Godin

Innovation should be on our daily to-do list. We are all heading towards the same goal, an upgraded future. Be creative, take risks, and act fast.

October 13

"There are three things extremely hard: steel, a diamond, and to know one's self."

— Benjamin Franklin

More often than not, most people believe that they know themselves fully. However, most will be surprised by how much they do not. Knowing one's self includes knowing who you are, what makes you, where you want to be in the future, how you will get there, and other factors. Once you get to it, you will realize that there is a lot more you need to learn about yourself.

October 14

"Never start a business to make money. Start a business to make a difference."

— Marie Forleo

I'm fascinated with the idea of helping others and how to make a bigger contribution. This doesn't come from small-mindedness or selfishness. Most of us want to have meaningful work and make a difference. What will you do to make a bigger impact? What are the barriers you'll face along the way? How will you overcome those barriers? How will you feel when you're making a difference?

October 15

"I think a hero is any person really intent on making this a better place for all people."

— Maya Angelou

We can all do so much more than we realize. What will we do with the opportunity?

October 16

"It isn't enough to talk about peace. One must believe in it. And it isn't enough to believe in it. One must work at it."

— Eleanor Roosevelt

Peace comes from strength. Bullying isn't the answer. If that's you, work on yourself and cut it out. Nobody benefits and everyone sees right through you.

October 17

"Peace brings with it so many positive emotions that it is worth aiming for in all circumstances."

— Estella Eliot

Tension and conflict are natural things for humans. They have probably always been here and they probably always will be. Peace is more difficult. It is not easy. It requires strength. It requires caution. It requires seeing the bigger picture and avoiding small-mindedness, power plays, and selfishness. While it is not easy, it is a goal this is worthy of pursuit. Where are some areas that you're struggling right now? What will you do to help move towards peace over conflict?

October 18

"Think big thoughts but relish small pleasures."

— H. Jackson Brown

Enjoying the little things in life and being content with less really is more in the long run.

October 19

"Each system is trying to anticipate change in the environment."

— Kevin Kelly

We all know that change is inevitable. We can relieve a lot of tension by acknowledging that change will happen, and then working to assure that we're best prepared for that change. We can decide to make the transition positive and view it as an improvement. We also must remember that there will be hiccups, speed bumps, and mistakes along the way. This is normal. It's all part of the process. Just think how amazing the change might be! It may be better than we initially anticipated.

October 20

"First you get the feeling, then you figure out why."

— Robert Pirsig

When we pause for a moment to examine our feelings and become aware of them, the next step is to understand the thoughts, actions, and behaviors that caused those feelings. Sometimes, it isn't possible to know why we are feeling the emotions or what caused them. What is more certain though, is that we can be proactive, and decide to consider diverse thoughts and act differently. Those are proven ways to bring different feelings into existence. We can feel however we'd like. All we have to do is figure out the combination of thoughts and actions that would lead to those feelings. How are you feeling? If you're not satisfied with your current feelings, how would you prefer to feel instead? What thoughts and actions will you need to alter?

October 21

"Being aware of your fear is smart. Dancing with your fear is the mark of a successful person."

— Seth Godin

Letting fear control us is not productive. Everyone feels fear. You can prevent it from taking over if you choose.

Feel it and acknowledge it. Then push past it. Push toward accomplishing what's most important to you. If it is worth doing, you will be proud of it once it is complete.

Are you feeling fear related to anything you were planning to accomplish recently? Do you write your goals and then glance at them regularly? How will you push past this obstacle so you can accomplish more things with confidence? You will succeed if you take action, believe, and do that very thing that makes you uneasy.

───•●•───

October 22

"Don't take it personally when someone turns you down. Assume they are like you: busy, occupied, distracted. Try again later. It's amazing how often a second try works."

— Kevin Kelly

We should remember that it can be incredibly powerful to learn to be more neutral on things. Sometimes, taking a neutral stance allows us to be less emotionally involved. This allows an opportunity for greater logic and curiosity. If we are neutral, and can see things without being too personally invested, we can see other possibilities. A world with more opportunities is better than a world with less of them.

October 23

"The bones and flesh and legal statistics are the garments worn by the personality, not the other way around."

— Robert Pirsig

We have to remember that statistics can be used in deceptive ways by people who have something to gain by doing so. It is always a good practice to remain somewhat skeptical when reading things before accepting it as a truth. Perhaps we should review the statistic's source before accepting it as truth and consider the author's real motive.

October 24

"It's not that optimism solves all of life's problems; it is just that it can sometimes make the difference between coping and collapsing."

— Lucy MacDonald

Optimism makes a huge difference. When in doubt, let's give things a chance knowing there are boundless opportunities ahead with those who have the right mindset.

October 25

"For myself I am an optimist — it does not seem to be much use to be anything else."

— Winston Churchill

If the alternative to optimism is pessimism, how can anyone argue that it's a better side of the fence to be standing on? Decide that you're committed to optimism and you will find things automatically get better.

October 26

"My optimism has helped me through some hard times. If you try to send out good things, good things come back to you."

— Jan Brett

When we give good energy freely into the world, we should remember to open ourselves to receive good energy in return, knowing that it usually comes back to us in ways we least expect. When we remember those experiences with gratitude, we compound the good that we may receive in the future.

October 27

"When I look at the future, it's so bright it burns my eyes!"

— Oprah Winfrey

We all have bad days, but what if each one of us was to view the future with this level of optimism and excitement?

October 28

"Don't be pushed around by the fears in your mind. Be led by the dreams in your heart."

— Roy T. Bennett

We can all move closer to our dreams if we spend some time to get clearer visions on what those dreams are, and move closer to it each day. Have faith in the future knowing that dreams do come true. Keep your fears at bay, keep moving forward, track your progress, celebrate your success, and keep on moving on.

October 29

"Motivation comes from working on things we care about."

— Sheryl Sandberg

We all want work that is meaningful and makes a difference. What motivates you? What do you care about most? Why? Are your choices in alignment with what you care about most? What changes might be necessary to give you a great degree of meaning?

October 30

"Happiness is not by chance, but by choice."

— Jim Rohn

If happiness is a choice — and I believe that it is — then we can always be happy. We regain our joy in life when we realize that what lies within us all is the conscious choice to decide what our future will be. We can be happy in the here and now. We decide and we act, and it materialized into the present. We should remember that others can't make us unhappy — the only one who can do that is ourselves. Since we deserve happiness, we will not let others bring us down, steal our joy, or affect our happiness. We choose to be happy. And so we are. We wish the same for everyone, and for all others.

October 31

"I can't change the direction of the wind, but I can adjust my sails to always reach my destination."

— Jimmy Dean

We all need to remember to roll with it. Adjust as the winds change. We can all learn to adapt more quickly. How will you adjust your sails so you reach your destination with ease?

November

November is fantastic. This month is the month that includes Veterans Day, Thanksgiving, Black Friday, and Cyber Monday. Huge shout outs to all the veterans out there! Thank you all for doing what you do.

There are only two months remaining in the year. Are you on-track to make this your best year? What are some of your best moments? What are some of the things for which you are most grateful? How has this year been different than you expected so far?

November 1

"What is the main event today? What do you want me to focus on today?"

— John C. Maxwell

What we focus on determines where our energy goes. If we have a clear vision of the future, and we put all of our focus and energy into it, combined with persistence and determination, there's almost nothing we can't do.

November 2

"A daily routine built on good habits and disciplines separates the most successful among us from everyone else. A routine is exceptionally powerful."

— Darren Hardy

Many of us recognize that it can be a bit boring to have a routine and that it's not much fun to have a rigid routine with little flexibility. We should also recognize that by establishing that routine, we really empower ourselves to accomplish the things that matter most to us.

November 3

"I have learned over the years that when one's mind is made up, this diminishes fear; knowing what must be done does away with fear."

— Rosa Parks

Having certainty makes most things easier. It is the uncertainty that is overwhelming and frustrating.

November 4

"You always reap what you sow; there is no shortcut."

— Stephen Covey

All too often in life, we are told that we can take shortcuts. Everyone offers us secrets to get more done, in less time. Here's how to save time. Here's how to make more money. Here's how to lose weight without dieting. What about if instead of all that, we go back to the basics? Do the hard work to achieve whatever goals you want to accomplish. It requires hard work, effort, and persistence. Don't take shortcuts. They are always more expensive in the end.

November 5

"You will regret many things in life, but you will never regret being too kind or too fair."

— Brian Tracy

How we treat others says a lot about us. Things like our outlook, what we believe in, and what we value. The world can always use more kindness and compassion. By following the Golden rule, we make the world a better place. What can you do to be more kind? Is there an area where you've been unfair to others in the past? How did that make you feel? How will you approach preventing that from happening in the future?

November 6

"Just as our eyes need light in order to see, our minds need ideas in order to conceive."

— Napoleon Hill

Where would we be without ideas? They are the root of all the great things we see around us every day. The best fast-food restaurants, the dope car model we drive, and everything around us stemmed from an idea. When we feed our minds with different ideas from different sources, we will be surprised by how many things our minds can come up with.

November 7

"Follow effective action with quiet reflection. From the quiet reflection will come even more effective action."

— Peter Drucker

As much as we need to act on what we want with speed, we must always think through things before doing them. Nobody wants to make the wrong life decisions or failures. Therefore, we must quietly reflect on things before we act on them. No matter how great the results of the actions may be, do not rush into things.

———•●•———

November 8

"For, in the end, it is impossible to have a great life unless it is a meaningful life. And it is very difficult to have a meaningful life without meaningful work."

— Jim Collins

The ability to do meaningful work, to do it well, to make a huge difference is fantastic. It is something that everyone should be able to experience regularly. Somehow, and sometimes we get lost along this path. Companies forget how to connect the work with its completion, or perhaps it is a complex or multi-step process. Job satisfaction can be diminished in situations like these. How can you make your work more meaningful? What impact does it have on others? How can you make an even greater impact by accepting more responsibility or providing a greater contribution? How will it make you feel once you have done so? What are the action steps required to get you moving in this direction?

November 9

"There is no end to the good you can do
if you don't care who gets the credit."

— Colin Powell

There are a lot of charitable activities happening everywhere. This is great because it shows that there are people out there who are willing to help others. However, how many of those people would do all these activities without taking the credit for it? We may never know. Authenticity comes from doing good without announcing it. Remember, do not let your left hand know what your right hand is doing.

November 10

"True fulfillment in life doesn't come from what we get, it comes from what we give."

— Marie Forleo

"Blessed is the one that gives, than he that receives." People are often recognized and remembered for their generosity. Mother Theresa is an icon that taught us that there is more to gain in giving than receiving. The person who is willing to give will never lack anything they need in life. The universe always provides to the generous.

November 11

"The cynics may be the loudest voices — but I promise you, they will accomplish the least."

— Barack Obama

Ever heard the saying, "The smallest dogs bark the loudest." Well, this is true for the dogs, but more so for we as human beings. Some people like to portray a positive image, someone who can do anything. Well, you will be surprised to find out that such people accomplish the least in life. Be humble and let your actions speak for you.

November 12

"If you could avoid all your mistakes, you'd miss everything you learned from them."

— Marie Forleo

I'm thankful for my mistakes mostly because of the things I've learned after making them. There have been many. They have been a great teacher and they serve as a great spirit guide for future me.

November 13

"I have found that among its other benefits, giving liberates the soul of the giver."

— Maya Angelou

We've all heard the adage that it is better to give than to receive. While it is nice to receive from others, by giving freely in a spirit of generosity and love, we open ourselves up to a whole new world of satisfaction and possibilities.

November 14

"When the power of love overcomes the love of power the world will know peace."

— Jimi Hendrix

Many people want power. They desperately want it, and seek it. Many try to steal it from others. Many try to put others down or point out others' blunders in order to elevate themselves. By doing so, they inadvertently ruin their opportunities because that's not a smart strategy. Eventually, it all comes to light. Only by doing the hard work, being mature, maintaining a positive attitude, and trying to get people to work together can we truly rise to a position of power.

November 15

"The future belongs to those who believe in the beauty of their dreams."

— Eleanor Roosevelt

Sometimes we feel as though our dreams are impossible to achieve. Others, we realize that the dream we had several years ago has come to us in the present. When we dream beautiful dreams, something comes alive inside each of us. More likely than not, we can move closer, and closer to the fulfillment of those dreams as each day passes. We need to have faith, believe in it, and be willing to commit and do the work. Do you believe in your dreams? Are you committed?

November 16

"In order to write about life first you must live it."

— Ernest Hemingway

Life is a constant stream of learning, growing, and experimenting. Making mistakes along the way. Learning what worked well, and what not to do next time. What we love and what we don't. We should ask ourselves, what is a life well lived? What are the components that make life the best? What brings us the greatest satisfaction and joy?

November 17

"The goal could be to become useful, remarkable and worth seeking out."

— Seth Godin

You are remarkable at something. That makes you special — really special as a matter of fact. Are you being truly you? Or, are trying to be more like someone else?

You should believe in yourself and all the special gifts that only you can offer to the world. You are great. Don't let anyone tell you anything different. When you offer yourself and your greatness to the world, you will be inevitably rewarded.

November 18

"One of the functions of an organization, of any organism, is to anticipate the future, so that those relationships can persist over time."

— Kevin Kelly

As I write this book in 2020, it's hard to avoid the topic of anticipating the future. This year has brought about such levels of unprecedented change. We all need to prepare for the future so that we can be ready for it. It is natural. In past years, the amount of change has seemed more manageable compared with the levels of uncertainty as a result of the pandemic. We didn't know COVID-19 was about to punch us. We could have done a better job assuming this level of uncertainty, and we could have done a better job preparing for unexpected challenges. The wisdom of our grandparents rings true today more than ever. Set some money aside for a rainy day. The truth is, we never know when we might need it.

———•●•———

November 19

"The place to improve the world is first in one's own heart and head and hands, and then work outward from there."

— Robert Pirsig

Transformation in the world around us comes from, or begins with shift inside our own minds and our own hearts. When we realize that everything that happens around starts with ourselves, we begin to see that we can influence and change the world around us and our very future by first being aware of what's going on inside our minds. If we want to improve the world, we have to get clear about what we want and what we expect to see in the future. We have to make sure that we are biased to think positively and optimistically. This is the foundation upon which our future is built.

November 20

"If you are deliberately trying to create a future that feels safe, you will willfully ignore the future that is likely."

— Seth Godin

As I write this book in 2020, one thing becomes apparent. There is a lot of uncertainty in the world. The year 2020 and the pandemic have been quite unusual. Being comfortable with the uncomfortable has been a great asset for me personally. No one really appreciates uncertainty, but knowing how to deal with it makes a huge difference. Only by stepping outside of our comfort zones can we truly embrace a future that is uncertain and adventurous.

November 21

"Experience is overrated. When hiring, hire for aptitude, train for skills. Most really amazing or great things are done by people doing them for the first time."

— Kevin Kelly

We often overlook the best candidates because we're blinded by a myth. The myth is that the person we hire needs to have experience. It isn't so. They can learn. You can't cure a bad (or negative) attitude. Find the right attitude and a person who has the aptitude to succeed, then see what they can do. They won't usually let us down.

November 22

"The more you look, the more you see."

— Robert Pirsig

We should always consider that we have an opportunity to slow down a little bit. Dig a little deeper. Ask more questions. To try to see things more thoroughly than we currently do. What will the result be if we make this decision? We might just find out that we gain some sort of additional information that makes an incredible difference in the world. What are some things that you feel like you should dig a little deeper in? How could you benefit by seeing things more clearly and completely?

November 23

"Do not anticipate trouble, or worry about what may never happen. Keep in the sunlight."

— Benjamin Franklin

We all recognize that things can go wrong along our journey. We spent a lot of energy on things that are possible, but unlikely to happen. What if we could use that energy to propel us forward, more quickly and effortlessly? What would be possible if we didn't have to worry about our troubles?

November 24

"Optimism is joyful searching; pessimism is a prison of fear and a clutching at illusionary safety."

— Kathleen A. Brehony

If you're a pessimist, let go. Let yourself out of the mental prison that is holding you back. Believe that anything is possible, have a positive attitude, and boldly move forward with focus and determination to improve.

November 25

"I am an optimist… I choose to be. There is a lot of darkness in our world, there is a lot of pain and you can choose to see that or you can choose to see the joy. If you try to respond positively to the world, you will spend your time better."

— Tom Hiddleston

What brings us true joy? How can we multiply that joy and share it with others? By making the decision and taking a proactive role, we bring light and become a part of a meaningful force that makes a better world.

November 26

"**Success is not final, failure is not fatal: it is the courage to continue that counts.**"

— Winston Churchill

When we keep moving forward, anything is possible. We should all work to learn from our mistakes and failures so that we don't repeat them. We can also save time and energy by learning from others' mistakes. The most important thing is to just keep moving forward — no matter what! That's what really counts.

November 27

"**Be thankful for what you have; you'll end up having more.**"

— Oprah Winfrey

We have a lot to be thankful about. Expressing gratitude is powerful habit, especially when done daily. I try to write three things down that I'm grateful for each day. How can we be more grateful for the things we have?

November 28

"Turn obstacles into opportunities and problems into possibilities."

— Roy T. Bennett

The obstacles are there to see how bad we want it. When we overcome those obstacles, opportunities come to us and we all achieve more.

November 29

"We must accept finite disappointment, but never lose infinite hope."

— Martin Luther King Jr.

Life comes with disappointments. No matter what, we have to remember to be hopeful and believe in future possibilities. It is easy to get sidetracked. It's also easy to get blown off course by the winds coming from the mouths of opinionated pessimists who would love nothing more than to bring us down to their level. When we rise, we empower ourselves, refuse to accept the negativity, and embrace an optimistic future that we, and only we can create by working together with others who are like-minded and dedicated to building a better world.

November 30

"A champion is defined not by their wins but by how they can recover when they fall."

— Serena Williams

Even champions fall. So we make sure we have a plan for how to get back up again. What's your plan? Are you prepared to fall? Will you learn something from it? Do you have the courage to get back on your feet again, and get back into the game?

December

December is here. Where has the time gone? We have many religious holidays this month, including the celebration of Christmas. Also, December is usually a celebration of Hanukkah, which can technically occur between late November to late December in the Gregorian calendar.

How has your year been so far? What are your must-do's that will get accomplished this month? What support will you need? What things do you need to be doing now to set yourself up for success next year? Be sure to take time to reflect on the things that went well this year and be grateful for every person you've encountered, each challenge you've faced, and all the success you have had. Celebrate your success and finish this year strong!

December 1

"The person who has a clear, compelling, and white-hot burning why will always defeat even the best of the best at doing the how."

— Darren Hardy

Having a compelling why, a vision of the future, is important. It gives us direction. The clearer the vision, the more likely it is that we will be able to achieve the outcome that we want.

The stronger and more intense the vision is, the more passion and energy we bring forward and can be used to bring that vision to life.

———•●•———

December 2

"Any fool can criticize, condemn and complain — and most fools do."

— Benjamin Franklin

They certainly do. They also have a tendency to drag others down while in the process of all that. It's easy to criticize, to complain. It's easy to be a squeaky wheel. Some people are just needy, and strongly desire to be the center of attention. They need a pat on the back. They want others to recognize how wonderful they are. They'll even tell you about it, over, and over, and over. I'm not one of those people. Let those who are critical do what they do best. I'll be out making a positive impact in the meantime.

———•●•———

December 3

"Positive expectations are the mark of the superior personality."

— Brian Tracy

Have you ever noticed that when you expect good things to happen, they normally do? How about when you expect bad things to happen — they normally happen, don't they? So much of what happens in the world is a direct result of our thoughts, beliefs, focus, and actions. Why not have positive expectations? What will be possible if we dedicate a lifetime to having a positive attitude and a bright outlook?

———•●•———

December 4

"There are no limitations to the mind except those we acknowledge."

— Napoleon Hill

Human beings are full of so much potential. As masters of the earth, we have the potential to achieve whatever we want. However, our minds can be our worst enemies by showing us limitations in our goals. We do not have to accept them. We ought to believe that we can conquer and achieve every goal we set. Set those mental limitations aside and push on.

———•●•———

December 5

"The first time you say something, it's heard. The second time, it's recognized, and the third time it's learned."

— John C. Maxwell

Repetition is said to be the mother of learning. People have a lot to think about. If we want them to take a particular issue seriously, we must be persistent in speaking about it. It may piss some people off, but that is how we know that the message is getting through. It may not be fun, but keep iterating.

———●———

December 6

"The key is not to prioritize what's on your schedule but to schedule your priorities."

— Stephen Covey

If everything is priority number one, nothing gets done on time. We all want to get everything done at one time. But, we must recognize that this is futile. It just doesn't make sense. Things have to be prioritized and the resources have to be allocated to get them done. Time is one of those resources. Without the right prioritization, strategic planning, and effective execution, getting everything done all at once will be impossible.

———●———

December 7

"The most important thing in communication is hearing what isn't said."

— Peter Drucker

It's easy to listen to respond. It's easy to make an argument with someone that your point of view is right. But, when we dig deeper and do our best to really hear what others are saying, what they are meaning, what they are feeling and experiencing, then we have a real opportunity to connect and make a bigger impact. By hearing and understanding more deeply, everyone wins.

December 8

"A culture of discipline is not a principle of business, it is a principle of greatness."

— Jim Collins

Discipline is not only for serious stuff but for life in general. Living a disciplined life is a guarantee for a successful future. Indiscipline may seem fun and attractive sometimes, but its results are not great. Discipline is the key to living in peace with everyone else, and earning their respect. With people's respect, nothing can stop you from reaching greater heights.

December 9

"Perpetual optimism is a force multiplier."

— Colin Powell

Life throws crazy things at us. At such times, only optimism can help us pull through. When we have hope that things will eventually work out, then they will indeed work out.

Pessimism will keep us stuck in our comfort zones, unable to accomplish anything substantial. But, with optimism, what can't we conquer?

———•●•———

December 10

"**Stand for something or you will fall for anything. Today's mighty oak is yesterday's nut that held its ground.**"

— Rosa Parks

Nothing began as it seems right now. Everything started from somewhere. Do not be swayed by the winds of opinions surrounding us. Stand firmly by what you believe, and you will bear fruit when the right time comes. Endeavor to build your character, cultivate ethical values, and be willing to uphold your beliefs when you face opposition from the world.

———•●•———

December 11

"**Sensitivity is a sign of strength. It's not about toughening up, it's about smartening up.**"

— Marie Forleo

A lot of people view sensitivity as a sign of weakness. However, it is the opposite, as it is one of the traits that make up a strong personality. A sensitive person is usually able to spot little things that often get ignored. Change comes from people being perceptive to ideas and working towards change. So, if you are sensitive, you are stronger than you think.

———•●•———

December 12

"Peace is liberty in tranquility."

— Marcus Tullius Cicero

When we have the freedom and ability to act as we wish, there is calmness in our thoughts. We all appreciate the times when we have the ability to do the things we would like to do. Making our own choices. Doing just what we want just how we want to. Doing it our way. If you had the ultimate power to choose, what would you choose to do with the majority of your time? Who would you do it with? What would your ideal day look like?

———•●•———

December 13

"You will face many defeats in life, but never let yourself be defeated."

— Maya Angelou

Though it may not feel like it, being defeated is really only a state of mind. Can any of us ever be defeated if we don't accept that as an outcome?

December 14

"With the new day comes new strength and new thoughts."

— Eleanor Roosevelt

There's something great about starting over again with fresh thoughts each morning. Something amazing and wonderful about beginning a new day with a positive attitude and an adventurous spirit. What will you do differently tomorrow? It's a fresh start!

December 15

"Only those who dare to fail greatly can ever achieve greatly."

— Robert Kennedy

We all have the capacity to achieve. Sometimes, people are afraid to act because they fear failure. Not acting or proceeding too cautiously feels much safer. Pushing forward, despite the fear of failure, makes most people uncomfortable. Remember, the discomfort is a sign of progress. When we venture outside our comfort zone, we have a real opportunity to grow and develop personally and professionally. Do you eagerly accept new challenges?

December 16

"Change is not a threat, it's an opportunity. Survival is not the goal, transformative success is."

— Seth Godin

We can try to survive, or we can decide to thrive. When we thrive, we contribute in a meaningful way to bring the future into the present.

December 17

"Much of outcomes research is a systematic attempt to exploit what is known and make it better."

— Kevin Kelly

If we all see opportunities to make things better, and we consistently work in that direction, we will almost certainly succeed. Clearly, we will make mistakes, and there will be times when we don't make things better, and that we inadvertently take a step backward unintentionally. But what is the alternative? We must always work to improve things, get better outcomes, and proceed forward. When we do, we make the world a better place. Everyone can do something. What will you do?

December 18

"Sometimes it's a little better to travel than to arrive."

— Robert Pirsig

The journey is often more fascinating than the destination. So then, we should enjoy all the things we experience — good and bad. Let's enjoy the things we learn and appreciate the people we meet. We can learn something from each of them. Enjoy the trip!

December 19

"Soon is not as good as now."

— Seth Godin

It's easy to put things off and procrastinate. Don't delay. We should act now. Let's do what we've been putting off. We will be proud of ourselves and feel really good about what we've done!

December 20

"Extraordinary claims should require extraordinary evidence to be believed."

— Kevin Kelly

These days, people get so much information from social media. It is always surprising to me just how incorrect this information is. There's still a chance that a professional journalist is putting out mis-information. But this problem seems to be growing worse each day with social media. Many people get their news from various social media sources. We have to remember that the information has not necessarily been adequately vetted. It also seems that the more outrageous something is, the more quickly it seems to spread. In my humble opinion, this is a particularly dangerous situation.

December 21

"**Stuckness shouldn't be avoided. It's the psychic predecessor of all real understanding.**"

— Robert Pirsig

Now and then, we are going to get stuck. We need to remember that this is a part of the process. It is natural to encounter barriers, speed bumps, and potholes along our journey. Eventually, we'll overcome all the barriers. Have faith. Stuckness is temporary. We should embrace it!

December 22

"One of the things I learned the hard way was that it doesn't pay to get discouraged. Keeping busy and making optimism a way of life can restore your faith in yourself."

— Lucille Ball

We should all remember that everyone gets frustrated or discouraged sometimes. We would be best served by remembering that those who achieve great things don't stay in that state for long. We can choose something different. Will we? What if we have an action plan for what we will do each time we feel discouraged? We can proactively choose to do something to change the state that gives us energy, makes us feel better, and helps reduce the time we stay there. Anything is possible with the right amount of optimism and energy!

December 23

"Optimism. It's not just a mindset, it is behavior."

— Larry Elder

What we think, we do. Think good thoughts. Do good things. Get better results. So simple, and so profoundly true.

December 24

"Don't let your failures define you —
let them teach you."

— Barack Obama

We learn more from our failures than from the things that we succeed in. As long as we learn a valuable thing along the way, it isn't really a failure after all... Is it? What if we celebrated all failures where we learn something, and use that knowledge to help others?

December 25

"While we may not be able to control
all that happens to us, we can control
what happens inside us."

— Benjamin Franklin

What if the inner work we do on ourselves is the force that really changes how we experience the world? What will we choose to change internally so that our external world must change to match our vision?

December 26

"It takes no more time to see the good side of life than to see the bad."

— Jimmy Buffett

It also feels better when you make the effort and learn to see the bright side of things. If we have the opportunity, why not choose to see the good? Those around us will surely notice, even though they may not say anything. But the difference will be noticed and appreciated, especially by those who we care about the most.

December 27

"The positive thinker sees the invisible, feels the intangible, and achieves the impossible."

— Winston Churchill

We all know of so many who only believe in what they can see. They focus only what's right in front of them at the moment. Often that's a smartphone or a social media post that keeps them from living up to their full potential.

———•●•———

December 28

"**Attitude is a choice. Happiness is a choice. Optimism is a choice. Kindness is a choice. Giving is a choice. Respect is a choice. Whatever choice you make makes you. Choose wisely.**"

— Roy T. Bennett

Thoughts lead to choices, which lead to actions, which leads to results. Doesn't it make sense then that we would spend more time being intentional about our thoughts and the future we're creating? Aren't we thinking thoughts that create the future?

———•●•———

December 29

"**If I cannot do great things, I can do small things in a great way.**"

— Martin Luther King Jr.

Small things done repeatedly well lead up to great things. When you repeatedly do the small things well, the end result most certainly will be good. So, you should pay attention to detail because the small things really do matter more than you've been told. When you do the small things right, you will get better results. You may even change the world for the better.

December 30

"Let us make our future now, and let us make our dreams tomorrow's reality."

— Malala Yousafzai

The future is nothing more or nothing less than we make of it. It's all up to us. We all have the power to create our own future that's amazing. Why not act with intention and dream it into existence?

December 31

"What you get by achieving your goals is not as important as what you become by achieving your goals."

— Zig Ziglar

We are transformed by the journey, not the accomplishment itself. It takes a while to learn this. But, without having the goal in the first place, we are less likely to take effective action. We're less likely to end up anywhere if we don't have a destination in mind. So, we need to set goals and head out. Just keep moving. We must believe and know that we will be positively transformed on our journey and that it will be an amazing journey indeed!

About the Author

Gregory Barton is a lifelong learner, a businessman, a writer, an aspiring imperfectionist, a practicing musician, a songwriter, an entrepreneur, a patriot, an armed forces veteran, a father, and a friend.

Gregory has decades of leadership and management experience in working with organizations of various sizes. He has a Masters of Business Administration (MBA) and various other degrees and credentials. He is passionate about his work with various organizations who want to be the best. He is a passionate lifelong learner. You can find Greg on Twitter at @GregBartonMBA.

One More Thing

In closing, I want to once again express my most sincere gratitude. Thank you for allowing me the opportunity to share my ideas. I truly hope you find these ideas valuable and that you will be able to use them in all your future endeavors. I wish you great health and the best success in business and in life.

Sincerely,

Greg

https://GregoryBarton.com